TALES FROM THE LOWER EAST

This provocative anthology of voices old and new from New York's East Village may offend those who like their literature like a tea setting in a museum—quaint, tidy and much too pretty to touch. Too bad.

Because these stories and poems reflect the turbulent recent history of New York's most dynamic avant garde community, a melting pot of artists, ethnics, poets, junkie, barflies, radicals, mystics, street people, con men, flower children, losers, screwballs, professional eccentrics, and non-conformists who now find the offbeat vitality of their neighborhood deluged by a flood of self-centered Yuppies intent on submerging the "EV" in a sea of condos, high fashion boutiques, cheesy art galleries and expensive restaurants that cater to well-groomed white people with an excess of money.

Fortunately, not everyone applauds the dinero-*grubbing mind-death ethos of the '80s, and the gentrification of the East Village is certainly not a* fait accomplis. *As the Tompkins Square Park riots of '88 proved, the polyglot, multi-racial community that gives the EV its pungent sense of excitement and urgency is far from ready to surrender to real estate speculators who wish to turn it into a sanitized, suburbanized sideshow shadow of itself.*

The writers in this volume—from Ted Berrigan and Herbert Huncke in the '60s to Emily XYZ and Richard Hell in the '80s—speak for the other East Village: the East Village of sex, drugs, rock and roll, poetry, art and radical poetry. They celebrate the not-always-admirable denizens of the EV who dare to live life on the edge, and dance with demons on the darker side of human experience.

A DAY IN THE LIFE

TALES FROM THE LOWER EAST

**An Anthology of
Writings from the
Lower East Side, 1940–1990**

Edited by Alan Moore & Josh Gosciak

Evil Eye Books
New York City 1990

The editors would like to thank the following publishers and magazines in which some of this material first appeared:

Ted Berrigan's "Everything Seems So Laid Back in the Park" appeared in the *Clown War* series edited by Bob Heman; Herbert Hucke's "Florence" appeared in *The Evening Sun Turned Crimson*, published by Cherry Valley Editions; Miguel Piñero's "A Lower East Side Poem" apeared in *La Bodega Sold Dreams*, Arte Publico Press; Lynne Tillman's "An East Village Romance" appeared in *Weird Fucks*, privately published; Peter Cherches' "Between a Dream and a Cup of Coffee" appeared in the *Red Dust* pamphlet series; Patrick McGrath's "Hand of a Wanker" appeared in *Blood and Water*, Poseidon Press; David Polonoff's "St. Mark's Horror" appeared in the *East Village Eye*, April 1986; John Farris' "Here" appeared in the *East Village Eye*; Gary Indiana's "A Pathetic Waltz" appeared in *Bomb*, 1986, No. 16; and finally, Ron Kolm's Duke & Jill stories appeared in *Between C & D*, Vol. 2, No. 1; *Public Illumination*, No. 32; *New Observations*, *Between C & D*, Vol. 2, No. 3, *Appearances*, No 13, *Avenue E*, No. 4, and *Public Illumination*, No. 33.

We appreciate these people, without whose help this book would never have seen light: Our designer Mark Michaelson, Mary Campbell who finished up, Robert Legault & Vicki Pederson for proofreading, Richard Fantina for type access and formats, Howard Seligman for backing, and Ron Kolm for his nudging.

First edition

Library of Congress Cataloging-in-Publication Data

A Day in the Life: Tales from the Lower East: an anthology of writings from the Lower East Side. Alan Moore, Josh Gosciak editors.

p.   cm.
ISBN 0-936556-22-6: $6.95

1. Lower East Side (New York, N.Y.)—Literary collections. 2. New York (N.Y.)—Literary collections. 3. American literature—New York (N.Y.) 4. American literature—20th century. I. Moore, Alan. 1951-   . II. Gosciak, Josh.
PS509.N5D39 1989
810.8'097471'09045—dc20   89-70790
                                                                   CIP

Evil Eye Books is distributed by Autonomedia, POB 568, Brooklyn, NY 11211-0568 • (718) 387-6471

TABLE OF CONTENTS

Introduction

Ted Berrigan, "Everybody Seems So Laid Back in the Park" 1

Herbert Huncke, *Florence* 3

Lynne Tillman, *An East Village Romance* 11

Tom Weigel, "Until the Real Thing Comes Along" 15

Tommy Trantino, *A Good Horse Laugh* 17

Tom Savage, "Helen on the Lower East Side" 21

Enid Dame, *Cafe Endgame* 23

Irving Stettner, *Tiger on Third Avenue* 35

Max Blagg, "Can I Get You Something?" 43

Ed Sanders, *The Muffins of Sebek* 47

Miguel Piñero, "A Lower East Side Poem" 61

Olivia Beens, *Watch the Closing Doors—Subway Stories* 65

John Farris, *Here* 69

Emily XYZ, *The Day John Left* 73

Ron Kolm, *Duke and Jill* 77

Patrick McGrath, *Hand of a Wanker* 85

Jorge Cabalquinto, "The Dog-Eater" 93

Joshua Whalen, *Venus* 95

Peter Cherches, *Between a Dream and a Cup of Coffee* 99

Carle Groome, *Auto da Fé* 107

Donald Lev, *Hegira to Avenue C* 117

Zoe Anglesley, "In the Garden of East" 126

Allen Ginsberg, *Notebook* 129

Richard Hell, From a novel in progress 137

Cookie Mueller, *Sam's Party* 147

Gary Indiana, *A Pathetic Waltz* 153

David Polonoff, *St. Marks Horror* 165

List of Illustrations 169

Introduction

BY THE EDITORS

WHEN WE STARTED COLLECTING MATERIAL for this book in 1986, the East Village was a much greener place. Money flowed, and talk about art, the gossip and money of art, became *the* talk of the town. The East Village *was* creating a new art, a new writing, and a new cadre of spokespeople. Magazines such as the *East Village Eye, Between C&D,* the *National Poetry Magazine, Avenue E* and *Public Illumination* were vehicles of literary change, much the same way as Ted Berrigan's *C*, published almost 20 years earlier, fired the new bohemia of the Lower East Side. Artists like Martin Wong, Kiki Smith, Bobby G, Seth Tobacman and Keiko Bonk set trends for art and the over sixty art galleries of the area during the '80s.

But the life of the East Village feeds on change—like the boom and bust of the '60s counterculture—and another occurred, almost overnight. In 1990 we have a bleaker landscape: a kind of suburban weekend punk shopping mall, where nearly all galleries have folded, and many writers and artists have moved on to cheaper environs, if not country pastures. What was once a thriving cultural community on the brink of global artistic fame has slipped into bare-bones anonymity, stripped of pretense and stalked by an angrier, more militant declassé culturati.

Like this Lower East, this endearing and rugged environment, our anthology evokes the peaks, troughs, ebbs and flows, from the 1940s to the 1990s, the record of hope and desire on the cutting edge of life and death.

Through these pages speak voices very alive though some are now dead; writers who've lived in this part of town when the most vital strains of American counterculture and avant-garde pulsed through. By your fireside you'll hear Ted Berrigan, the "original East Village poet," start with a shout; Herbert Huncke, a beat-era literary figure too little heard relates a strange love story. Novelist Lynne Tillman's tale is a frank evocation of the '60s: "I was a slum goddess in college ... 'cunt breathing free.' "

Enid Dame's narrator, in a tale set in the same psychedelic-era East Village, lives with the clutch of an anxious family hovering about as their daughter adventures. *Stroker* publisher Irving Stettner walks the neighborhood's avenues with a true local's aplomb; bartender-poet Max Blagg sardonically takes an order. Ed Sanders' dense, colorful tale evokes the magical bohemia that should have been, even if NYC now really is more like Olivia Beens' gallery of harrowed characters.

The late Nuyorican bard Miguel Piñero's "streets are hot and feed off those who bleed to/ death ..." These hard-living, downtown homeboys meet up with John Farris to lay in some "lumps & bumps," while Emily XYZ's benumbed young heroine gets her share of useless love. Ron Kolm's "Duke and Jill do drugs ... Bad things keep happening to them." Not so bad as Patrick McGrath conjures up for a nightclub—the thinly disguised Pyramid—in a gothic-style horror tale, nor so relentlessly miserable as the life of Jorge Cabalquinto's dog-eater, seen through the eyes of a young boy.

Joshua Whalen loses his "Venus" in a whirl of police work, the kind that set the stage for the East Village of the nineties—the "Alphabet Town" of gentrification. Peter Cherches moves through his enigmatic rounds, Richard Hell' rock 'n' roll doper struts his jaunty, pitiable hour; maybe only last night he was at Cookie Mueller's "Sam's Party," and just missed his brush with death. Meanwhile, in his apartment and straight down on the street Carle Groome's hero watches street life explode into his doped and loveless existence.

Donald Lev's man just wants to run a bookstore, living the literary *vie boheme*, when the Lower East was a refuge for scholars; Gary Indiana's globetrotter wonders at the dissolution of what he called community and ponders his future in letters. Allen Ginsberg's "Notebook" excerpts add to this poetry of daily life his journal notations of life on his block. David Polonoff rounds out the woeful count as he outlines the haunting of a yuppie couple by ghosts of an East Village past.

This book is about a place. For anyone who's passed through its portals, that place is at once real and a fiction. The reality of homelessnes, drugs and violence, and the fiction of the American Dream—the new, connecting with others—merge art with the reality of the Lower East.

Writers are not journalists; short stories don't tell the story, nor do poems deliver the news. It is rather the raw life of the struggle to be living as s/he wants that shines through in these tales—the thrill of it, the fancy schemes, the fireworks, the regrets. Shambling through these disparate works is a single figure, a person living by choice in a place that breathes the metier of creative freedom. No one condones or disapproves, none interferes in the exercise of free will; fate brings events to an end. The dark shadows in this book are starkly drawn, and in them ancient human evils claim their victims. And the living always have something to say about it.

Everybody Seems So Laid Back in the Park

BY TED BERRIGAN

Marie in her pin-striped suit singing
"Where Have All The Flowers Gone?" in German
Hot alfalfa covers the ground of Lilac Park.
"C'mere for a second!" shouts the invisible
Old lady. She crosses the park in a hat of nylon.
Marie falls down, still singing.
I see a woman with a baby running.
Two Africans in turbans wiggle their hips.
Marie cries & yawns for her audience.
Marie lights an envelope with matches.
Frisbees fly in the hot sun.
"Try it again."
A very pale orange is sitting under the baby birds.
The community lightens, five o'clock, lifting my heart
    to a place.

Florence

BY HERBERT HUNCKE

FLORENCE's PAD — EVENING. FLORENCE JUST CAME in. She is looking well and a bit agitated, perhaps unsure, although I seldom apply insecurity as a measure of what to expect from one's behavior. She is a strangely beautiful woman. She is and has been good to me. I am not sure exactly what our combination is apt to produce. I have, way in back, a sense or perhaps an awareness of guilt, believing my behavior toward her has been tinged with selfishness and I have treated her unkindly.

She and I have been violent on many occasions. In one instance, I became dramatic; screaming at her, forcing her back into a corner, falling over a chair, yelling "I'll kill you—kill you. Shut the fuck up please—please stop" half choking her, half insane wondering how in hell I'd become involved with her in the first place. We' both had habits and it had all started with bickering and complaining about trouble getting a hit. On other occasions I struck her. We yelled and argued; snide remarks, sarcasm, hate, general shit.

Florence is a very open and love giving person. She is extremely hip, having moved thru several wild and great scenes as far back as Charlie Parker early years in the city. She has been in touch with the jazz scene—digging music and musicians, active and swinging people, hustlers and knock around people. She likes living and has a direct way of accepting all experience. She is neither bitter nor hostile. She is a trifle reserved when meeting people, using a fairly hard set of so-called ethical evaluations while growing accustomed to the person. Yet she is without illusion and regardless of the manner or sudden awareness of having picked up the short end of a deal, or having become stuck with it, she takes it in stride and continues to know the person or people, explaining their seeming deceit or treachery rationally and with a kind of understanding.

She is cognizant of a basic truth within herself and she tries living close to that awareness.

We lived together last year beginning about April. We met at Arnie's pad on Houston Street. She came in during a session of amphetamine and pot smoking among a group of manipulative people moving around mixing solutions, painting, searching among boxes and in corners, behind hangings, passing from room to room. She wanted to cop some horse and sounded on Arnie who in turn introduced us. She startled me a little and I began digging her surreptitiously wondering how she fell in and what she was doing getting straight. She didn't, in a sense, look like what one might unconsciously associate with schmeck. Arnie gave her stuff and asked me to hit her. While we were getting the hit, we talked briefly. She said she was anxious to get away from the scene, get back to her place. When we had finished, she thanked me and gave me a kind of running verbal patter about how easily I had given her a hit, what trouble she sometimes had and suggested maybe I stop by her place with Arnie. She departed and I was attracted to her and hoped perhaps I'd see her again.

Not long afterwards, Arnie and I were out walking and just sort of knocking around the streets and, being near 16th Street where she lived, we visited her. She was living in a small but oddly comfortable room and her actions were seemingly sure and had an air of being productive. She was charming and I felt she liked me. She invited us to have dinner with her the next evening; we planning of copping some shit, relaxing in her place and eating.

She has and has had for the past several years a great little companion and pet, a sharer of woes and love, a very wise and good poodle, who is definitely a personality and individualized in all senses of the word—Florence's little dog. Florence named the little dog Pooka, explaining a pooka is a legendary little creature of one's own imaginings, sort of made to order, existing in Irish mythology. She and Pooka are inseparable and much of Florence's desire to be demonstrative and affectionate is directed toward Pooka.

The dinner was fine. Florence is a good cook and doesn't let the physical effort required to organize a good meal and prepare it drag her; she can cook good things to eat. We all got high, laughing, talking, exchanging stories and ceasing, for the moment, to be weighed down with paranoia. We passed several hours and Arnie finally cut out alone. Florence talked with me about her loneliness and said she liked me and would like overcoming to some degree her aloneness in my company. I was lonely also and although I wasn't sure we would become or might become close, I liked her with a feeling of respect and enjoyed her considerate little overtures of affection. Florence took care of me and was unselfish, sharing everything with me and materially giving far more than I. She supplied money and I copped. We shared our junk equally. The time accumulated and Pooka, Florence and I drew closer.

We decided to move and Florence and I walked the hot July streets looking for a new spot. Florence was against moving to the lower east side. Florence and I both didn't want to be invaded by amphets heads. I simply didn't want the responsibility of having to be constantly on the alert, perhaps protecting our possessions (or at least Florence's). Florence didn't want that kind of excitement. We confined our looking to the west side. With the help of an ad in the Village Voice, we located a small but great little place on 9th Avenue and 14th Street. Sneaking most everything out of Florence's old place to avoid paying the last week's rent, we became established after several trips carrying boxes and suitcases, odds and ends such as a plant of green leaves, dishes, pots and pans, a couple of lamps, a painting Arnie had done which he gave to me which was huge and square and filled with bright tempera tones of royal blue, yellow green, red, amber, of happy cartoon-like figures of St. George and the dragon, the five or seven headed Hydra, an active little angel hanging in the sky above the scene acting as a kind of referee or guardian type role. All the figures had wings and St. George carried a yellow sword. It took the entire night to complete the move.

Florence had had a bank account when we first met and after the account ran out and we were uptight for money, we would cash a phony check against the account. Later, this became our only source of income and we both spent long daily conferences about cashing checks—who we could hit, whether we should write for ten or fifteen, twenty or thirty-five, figuring each possibility for all it could offer. It took us no time to run through the local stores where either of us were known. Florence had a wider range than I, since almost all these places knew her only as a nice little lady who sometimes had to cash a check. We tried any and all leads. Our habits had increased and we were living comfortable. Florence received a weekly unemployment check that we used to pay rent, stock in groceries and cop three or four five dollar bags. Our connection was on the east side and the first thing we would do in the morning of the check delivery was to rush to the check cashing store, get the bread, grab a taxi and head to see our man and get straight.

Gradually we began cashing checks with close acquaintances and friends. Florence visited people she had known for years in Long Island, Astoria and Brooklyn, while I began calling on people I had met on a more conventional level. I burned several good friends. This through most of the summer. At one point we lost our connection—who had decided to pack everything in, kick his habit, get off the scene. We had been good customers and before leaving he arranged to meet a half load connection (a half load consisting of fifteen bags for twenty-five dollars). Between us we averaged ten bags a day and we planned selling the rest.

We started, at this point, copping half loads every day, finally copping as often as three or four times a day. I began getting customers and had a good business going. Still, we never managed as efficiently as was required and our lives became a steady grind of scheming and conniving, shooting more junk, finding fault in each other. We became careless about our dealings with people who knew our address and they came threatening and pounding on the door demanding money, promising to cut us, and get even. We were behind on rent and had to get out.

Florence got her weekly check and we sneaked out again. Clive and Erin helped us. We had acquired a great little black cat we named Mister, and we had Pooka. Somehow we managed to get out with clothes and a few odds and ends. We stayed with Erin and Clive a couple of days and then found a room on Tenth Street just off the Bowery or Third Avenue.

I had been in contact with an old colored junk pusher. He was anxious to set up a business arrangement on the lower east side. We discussed plans and he agreed to paying a month's rent for Florence and I and himself and a little chick he was taking care of. His name was Charlie and he had been in the business a long time. He would supply the merchandise and I would handle the business.

We located a spot and we moved in. Our location was on Tenth Street near First Avenue. The pad was a sharp spot and we lived there from July—maybe August, until October. By late September, I had a good business going. We lived comfortably, shot all the junk we wanted (or at least we kept our habits going steadily without too much hassle). Toward the beginning of October, Florence and I began having differences of opinion. It began with drugs, or at least, I became increasingly more annoyed and spoke nastily. Florence was irritated also and became more tense. My business sense is not keen and Florence complained of Charlie not coming through fairly. She was getting her check and buying food and copping extra bags from Charlie. She was disgusted and wanted to get out. She began using goof balls and getting completely stoned. Much of her frustration was directed at me and I became unpleasant. Either Clive offered his place on Avenue A and 12th Street or Florence asked him if she could stay there. She moved her things out. Then she called me to please bring over a bag and the works and please hit her because I knew how impossible it was for her to hit herself. I made the run, delivered the bag, cooked up the fix and hit her. She had taken several Doriden and when the stuff hit her she sort of zonked out. I shook her and made some kind of contact, asking if she had taken goof balls and she lied and said she hadn't. I couldn't get hung up with her at that point, going over each time she called and shooting her up, having her collapse, with doubt in mind about whether she had O.D.'d or not. She staggered over, Pooka by her side and stood in front of the building rocking back and forth, staggering away finally back to Avenue A. This all settled into a regular routine and then one afternoon she had convulsions. It was my first experience with a physical condition where there was violent muscular contortion, a stiffening of the body, quivering rigidity, gurgling, gasping breath, dribbling streams of saliva hanging from the lips, jerking straining black eyes, fear and confusion. I held her. I spoke with her. I pleaded with her, tried placing a silver spoon on her tongue—something about not swallowing her own tongue. I cradled her in my arms, trying every way to calm her and help her. I succeeded finally, partially bringing her round and she had another seizure, not as bad as the first nor as long. My own nerves began calming a little bit and I could function a bit more effectively.

The days passed somehow and things remained tense and uneasy. A cat burned me on the streets. Called me requesting four or six bags, arranged where to meet me and when I got there, there were two cats, one standing in the doorway. We passed him and I caught a glimpse of him at about the time the cat stuck a knife at me, coming on hard saying "Come on man—give me the shit. I don't want to fuck around—give it to me." I was carrying it in my hand and sort of passed it to him, trying to pull away and keep aware of the whole scene. There was no difficulty and as soon as he had the shit, they split. The cat in the doorway bounced out and cut past me joining his partner and they faded into the night as I returned to the pad. I discussed it with Charlie and he felt we had been lucky it hadn't happened sooner. It happened again about a week or week and a half later. Another pair of cats. They also beat me for a ten dollar bill.

One morning Charlie and I were just getting up—his chick had been gone a few weeks and Florence was off the scene. We were alone. Charlie was making a phone call and we were preparing to get organized for the morning fix. I was sitting on the edge of my bed, just having finished lighting a cigarette, when the apartment door was wrenched open and in walked two members of the narcotics squad. They had received a tip on Charlie and he was supposed to have sold to an agent on some earlier date. They were easy going enough, snooping around, making wisecracks, locating our stuff in the drawer—our works, finding a bag in my wallet and arresting me for possession. We were permitted to dress. Charlie explained we hadn't gotten straight and we would probably be getting sick and asked if they would let us cook up. They didn't let us cook up but instead gave each of us a bag and when we got to the station house, we snorted. It held me together through the day.

They offered me a proposition concerning Avenue C and lining up pushers and helping them to clean up the avenue. They said they would arrange a bail of twenty-five dollars cash for me and I'd be on the streets that night. I agreed and was released and told to appear in court the following Wednesday.

As soon as I left the court building I headed for a place to cop. I copped and went up to the pad. I felt it would be wise to split. Many of my customers were still ringing the phone—some had copped other places and hadn't waited. I had no other connection than Charlie and he handled the bread and source of supply. I stayed two and a half days, uneasy and unable to get anything practical going. Florence had told me I could stay with her and I packed my cases and deposited them and myself with Florence. We talked of my kicking—I could use her technique. Taper off with goof balls. She would go and see her doctor, have him make out a prescription for fifty Doriden. I don't know if I believed I would kick my habit but at least I could cut down. I felt beat and defeated and agreed to her suggestion. We got everything in order, copped one more bag of heroin, did it up, downed two or three Doriden and I remember nothing more until I awakened in the emergency ward at Bellevue. I was bewildered and knew nothing of how I had gotten there. They told me my wife was also in the hospital and that we had set fire to the mattress and probably would have a touch of smoke poisoning. The police had brought us in an ambulance.

I stayed in the hospital a week. Florence and I had a short visit. She had been examined and they wished to take X-rays. She was an ill woman probably in need of surgery. We kept indirectly in touch by way of attendants coming down from her floor, delivering packs of cigarettes. Meanwhile, the day of trial arrived and passed without my hearing from the police. I felt sure they had been notified and my arresting detectives would be up there to pick me up. The next day I was released.

Erin came up and picked me up and took me to her place. Erin had some amphets which she kindly gave me. I did a lot of writing, sleeping, talking and staying straight with amphets. I had lost my horse habit but was weak and beat.

Something happened with me concerning Florence and the hospitals. When she called to ask why I hadn't visited her and to tell me of her pending operation, I was unable to respond and I accused her of dramatics and hurt her feelings until toward the end of our conversation she said "Fuck you Huncke" and after a short outburst of anger and hurt feelings she hung up.

Time passed and Erin and Clive wanted the privacy of their apartment. Thru circumstances, I ended up living with Noah and Paul on Third Street. Christmas came, New Year's and one day about eleven o'clock in the morning (I was alone—Noah and Paul were gone) there was a knock on the door. I asked who was there; a strange man's voice replied "do you know this woman—she says she lives here." I opened the door to find Florence swaying in front of me.

I looked at the man and said "I don't know her" (and shut the door in her face). All was quiet for a few minutes while I stood beside the door, my mind in a whirlwind of thought, shame, rationalization, sadness and anger at Florence who was obviously goofed up on barbiturates. She knocked again and I opened the door, rushed at her, shaking her and telling her to stay out of my life, I couldn't take her in, I had no real business being there myself. She argued with me. She fell, losing her glasses. She sat on the top step refusing to leave and I hit her, hissing at her to get out of the building away from me. She cowered on the step holding her arms and hands up around her head in protection and said "I'm going." Then she looked at me and yelled "You fool—you fool." I went into the pad and shut the door. Several neighbors had stepped out to see what had happened and they helped get her under way.

I thought of it all day and my mind remained conscious of it for a long time.

Events occurred—changes—another jail term for me and then back on the scene in June. I heard from friends Florence was around and looking well. We encountered each other on the street. She was the same Florence I first met—bright-eyed and forgiving and lonely.

She invited me to visit and stay with her. She tries to make things comfortable. She has bounced back up on her feet. She wishes to share with me.

I sincerely love Florence. We have shared a strange companionship. She is my friend.

My behavior has been bad. Somehow I behave with Florence as I never have with anyone else.

I want only to be peaceful. I want to be free with her and never again become involved in violence.

I am relaxed and comfortable. Pooka is looking great and chases her ball, is petted, wags her tail, generally adjusts to the scene. She is affectionate, playful, a little bit naughty now and then but a little impish beauty.

Florence is sleeping. She arranged everything for me before lying down so that when I am ready for sleep all I'll find necessary to do is undress and fall into bed.

I'm here but it is really Florence's pad. It is bright and neat and fresh and white. It gives off a kind of sparkle and I am afraid my presence alone will serve to dim the light.

An East Village Romance

BY LYNNE TILLMAN

I WAS A SLUM GODDESS AND IN COLLEGE. HE LOOKED something like Richard Burton; I resembled Liz. It was, in feeling, as crummy and tortured as that.

George had a late night restaurant on St. Marks Place. I'd go in there with Hope, my roommate; we'd drink coffee, eat a hamburger. Fatal fascination with G. behind the counter—his sex hidden, but not his neck, his eyes, his shoulders. He called me "Little One." "Little one," he'd say, "why are you here? What do you want?"

I'd sit at the counter with hot coffee mug in hand, unable to speak, lips pressed on teeth, teeth pressed in heart, heart located in cunt, inarticulate. Michael said I was "cunt breathing free."

Jose was George's best friend and George had a Greek wife who was not around. The guys and I hung out together. $1 movies at the Charles. Two-way conversations between the artists (they were both sculptors) while I hung, sexually, in the air. Jose had a red beard, George had no beard, just greyish skin in the winter.

Little One he'd say what do you want? He'd trace a line on my palm as if it were a map of my intentions.

Still, with so much grey winter passion, no fucking. Night after night, nights at the counter, count the nights. I met his wife who dried her long black Greek hair in the oven. They are separated. It is a recent separation and I am passionately uncaring. I am in love. I take trips with other people to places I can't remember. I spend hours talking with an older woman called Sinuway who gives me a mirror to remind me I am beautiful. She disappears.

Jose reminisces about the fifties when beatniks roamed the streets. In those days George made sidewalk drawings. One time Jose recounted, "George was very drunk—very drunk, heh George—and drawing a young girl's portrait. For hours and hours because he'd fallen asleep behind the easel, his face blocked by the paper. Finally George collapsed at her feet, right on his face, nothing on the paper. Remember George?" Stories like these pass the time. Weeks pass.

George, Jose and I were in George's room and Jose put a ring on my finger then left the room. George and I were alone. He undressed me and placed his hand on the place between my breasts. He undressed me in the doorway. He unbuttoned everything and fucked me. It went fast, after so many weeks, fast, like a branch breaking off a tree. The time had come. It was a snap.

"I want to write a poem," he said, his cock still hard. "Oh, I don't mind," I said, dressing as fast as I could. I wanted to be indifferent, not to burden him with my lack of sophistication. He had an ugly look on his face. Perhaps he was thinking about his recently separated wife drying her hair in the oven while he fucked a young woman.

Back on St. Marks Place, I headed home, thinking that this might be reason enough for suicide. All that time, that perfunctory fuck, that poem he would write. It was all over. I phoned Susan who still lived at home; her life wasn't plagued with late night restaurants. What would you do I asked. Forget it she said, it's not important.

Later that night Hope and I went out again and I met Bill. He traced a line from my palm up my wrist all the way to my elbow.

A VERY QUIET GUY

Bill and I left Hope and went to the Polish Bar not four doors from George's late night restaurant. Beer ten cents a glass. We drank and drank; I told Hope I'd be home soon and wasn't.

Somehow we were upstairs in somebody's loft. Bill had red hair and brown eyes. He was very tall and wore a flannel shirt. We made love all night long, this kind of sleepless night reassuring. His rangy body and not much talking. He'd keep tracing that line from my palm to my elbow, the inner arm. He disarmed me. It was easy to do.

Early morning at the B & H dairy restaurant with red faces like Bill's hair. Breakfast with the old Jews in that steamy bean and barley jungle. Romance in the East Village smelled like oatmeal and looked like flannel shirts. Our smell in the smell of the B & H. George and Jose walk in and it was a million years ago, our weeks of grey passion and one snappy fuck. Sitting with Bill, so easily read, I smile at them. George looks guilty and embarrassed. I feel wanton and he is history.

Bill and I started to go together. He told me about his wife from whom he was separated. She was on the other coast. That seemed like a real separation. Bill was quiet and often sat in a corner. I thought he was just thinking. I introduced Michael, the first hippie I knew, to Nancy, my best friend. We spent New Year's together on 42nd Street, Nancy kissed a cop, the guys pissed on the street and Michael pissed in the subway.

Bill and I started a fur eyeglass case-making operation which I was sure would catch on. We convinced Charly, owner of the fur store on St. Marks Place, that those scraps of fur would make great eyeglass cases. A fur sewing machine was rented and placed in the basement of the fur store. Bill and I passed nights sitting side by side, silently, in old fur coats, stitching up cases which never did get sold. Bill grew more and more quiet.

My father had his first heart attack. The subways were on strike and I took long walks to Mt. Sinai in my fur coat to visit my father in the intensive care unit. That night I couldn't go home and slept on the couch at Nancy's mother's apartment. In the morning Nancy stood by the couch, anxious because the sheet covered me completely, like a shroud, and she wondered how I could breathe.

One night Bill fucked me with energy. Spring was coming and so was his wife he told me later. I stormed out of the fur store, yelling that I would never see him again, and fumed to the corner where I stood, having nowhere to go. That fuck was premeditated—wife here tomorrow, do it tonight. I turned back and returned to Bill and Michael who said, "We knew you'd be back. You're too smart for that."

We went to Nancy's and suddenly I was sick, throwing up in her mother's toilet bowl. Bill held my head, my hair. He took me to my apartment and made me oatmeal. Left me propped up in bed with a pile of blankets and fur coats over me. Three days later, I awoke, my flu over.

His wife had a beautiful voice and was as tall as he was. And while I could get him out of my system he couldn't get out of the system. He didn't want to resist the draft; he desperately wanted to pass the tests, especially the mental test. When he received his notice telling him he was 1-A, he tried to kill himself. Slit his wrists. Last time I remember seeing him he was sitting in an antique store, rocking, near the window. We waved to each other.

Until the Real Thing Comes Along

BY TOM WEIGEL

Everywhere there are blonds full of their blondness
as dayglow orange triangle remind
me of lip brushes lost in the amber film
of new condominiums shoulders rubbing the corners
with brass livid with rain,
as hasty & postindustrial, the new Avenue A
is lulling me to sleep with its pristine air
of antique platters and demitasse cups
& its portly beef-eating joggers
trundling around Tompkins Square Park
in the reveries of the gentrified
snapping me into the clean future
like a school child's vision
of mysterious days to come
as before the grail there was sight,
or so I dreamed it—
today on Candlemas's waxen snow
what's up in the air is down here
Beowulf aloft in the blue
Wash of winter's plates
while the cat in the window
sees the radio going by.

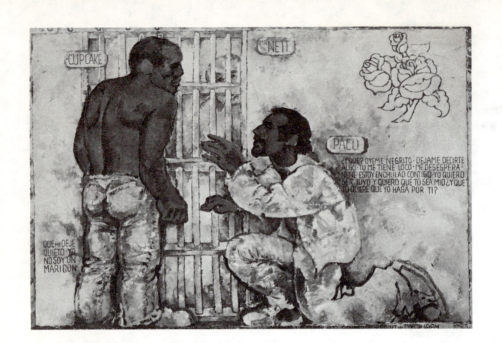

A Good Horse Laugh

BY TOMMY TRANTINO

WHEN I WAS YOUNG I USED TO BE A BIG drunk and I was always out on a bat drinking at whatever bar I happened to be passing. One night, as I was making my rounds on Second Avenue, I stopped at the Hi-Ho Silver Club. (This was about 24 years ago; the joint is probably off the map by now.) Sawdust on the floor. A piano player who played between the keys and sang like he had a mouth full of matzoh. Sign behind the bar said, "IN GOD WE TRUST, ALL OTHERS PLEASE PAY CASH." A bloody bucket. Fights all the time. Broads with more miles on them than any highway. You know the kind of joint. The kind of joint that when you walk in and step up to the bar you'll see a big hat sitting on it full of money. The kind of joint that you don't have to say what's up, because when you order your drink, there's going to be somebody who's gonna tell you. I ordered a triple Scotch. Before the dink came, one of the guys standing nearby asked me if I thought I could make a horse cry. "There's a horse in the back, if you want to try," he said.

"Why would I want to make a horse cry?" I asked, drinking my triple down and ordering another, chasing it with a Camel.

"To win the hatful of money," the guy told me, pointing to the hat and winking at the crowd that was starting to gather around me.

"Put ten bucks in the hat and you can try," the bartender said. "But as you can see, there's a lot of ten dollar bills in the hat. Ain't nobody been able to do it yet," he said.

"If I can't make a goddamn horse cry, I don't deserve this drink," I said and dumped it down the old gullet, smooth as can be. Everyone jibed. Bets went back and forth on all sides. But I was the only one taking me. "Is the horse a thoroughbred?" I asked.

"Does it matter?" the bartender said.

"Just making conversation," I replied.

"The drinks are on the house!" the bartender laughed as everyone stepped to the bar and I walked out back to the horse.

I was back in five minutes. I went over to the bar and I picked up the hat full of money. "Whoa! Where you goin' with *that*?" the bartender said, and I was quickly surrounded.

"You said if I made the horse cry, I win the pot, right? Well, go out back and see for yourself—the horse is crying his eyes out," I said.

The bartender sent three guys out back to check and they came running back with their eyes bugged out. They told the bartender and everyone else in the bar to go see for themselves, but the damn horse was back there crying like a baby. Everyone in the joint looked at me, their mouths little o's as I took the money and left—after buying a round for everyone of course.

Tempis foots it. About six months later, still on the bat that would carry me to prison forever, I stopped by the Hi-Ho Silver Club again. I was recognized immediately. It seemed like I'd never left. Same place; same people. The only difference this time was they were betting on making the horse laugh and nobody was winning because the hat was full of ten dollar bills again. I was baited. I quickly drink two triples down. Then I put the ten bucks into the hat and walked out back again, this time to make the horse laugh. And I did. The same guys ran out back and ran right back and said the horse was laughing so hard it was unbelievable. This time everybody in the joint ran out back to see for themselves. They came back in utter disbelief.

I took the money. "Drinks for everybody," I said. Everyone wanted to know how I did it. "My lips are sealed," I said, "except for this." And I drank my drink.

"First you make the horse cry, then you make the horse laugh—you gotta tell us how you did it," the bartender said, "Or you ain't leaving here alive."

"All right," I said, "I'll tell. But first—another round for everyone, including me."

"Here's to better days," the bartender said, toasting. Cheers. Everyone guzzled. Then everyone grew quiet and stood there, surrounding me on all sides, waiting.

"Okay, now tell us how you got the horse to cry," the bartender said.

I lit up a cigarette. I blew a smoke ring. Then another. "How?" I said. "Very simple. First to make the horse cry, I told him that my prick was bigger than his. And boy, did he cry."

"Then how did you get him to laugh?" the bartender said. "I took it out and showed it to him," I said.

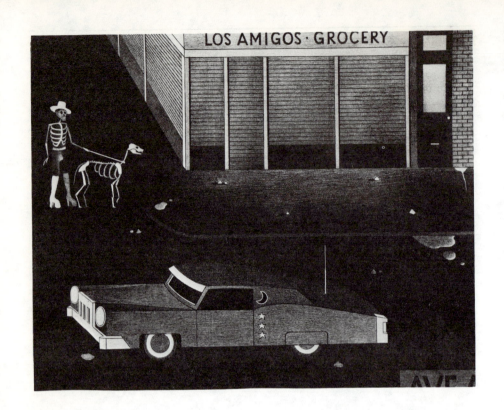

Helen on the Lower East Side

BY TOM SAVAGE

First her name's Helena
Then Elena. Then she switches back.
Meanwhile, she's taking off her clothes
To a ghettoblaster beat.
As she moves into and out of bodies
With her fancy eyes, she cries
With joy. She also knows
One other little trick. She'll be
Man or woman at your command.
She comes with the necessary attachable parts,
As switchable as thunder,
As loud as the junkie's scream.

Cafe Endgame

BY ENID DAME

IT WAS 1967. HALF THE WORLD WAS ON THE PILL. PEOPLE talked knowingly of the sexual revolution. Susan slept briefly with unkempt young men, and felt she was taking part in the great movements of her time.

Susan, just out of college that May, had come to New York to be a writer. And she did write a surprising amount, at first. Mostly, she wrote letters to her mother.

Susan's feelings about her mother were deep, but obscure. She felt that both women were, in some undefined way, conspirators against the rest of the world, which consisted of their Baltimore neighbors, the Waxman relatives, and, most particularly, Susan's father, a flat-faced, pragmatic man, who managed a variety store called "Bargain World" on the edge of a black neighborhood. The name of this store had infuriated Susan for years. "It's not a *world*, it's a *store*," she had insisted, ever since sixth grade, sometimes contemptuously, sometimes on the verge of tears. Her father refused to see her point. "Listen, I didn't name it," was his invariable response.

Mrs. Waxman disliked Bargain World for another reason: it sold ugly goods. She preferred to buy her dishes, cooking utensils, and household ornaments at elegant department stores like Hutzler's, or antique shops down on Howard Street, or at garage sales out in the country, where you could find wonderful gold-freckled sherry glasses, or interestingly crazed cream pitchers. All Susan's father's relatives thought Susan's mother was, to say the least, a little cracked herself. "Imagine, she doesn't even use the discount!" a shocked Aunt Sheila had once declared, in Susan's hearing.

When very young, Susan felt she must protect her fragile mother from the rough handling of the blunt-fingered aunts and cousins. But, actually, Susan's mother was very good at protecting herself. She did this by withdrawing into a vague, non-threatening haziness. Like a magician with his all-purpose veil, she could make difficult situations disappear. She refused to see insults, or hear innuendos; often she'd insist on taking a sarcastic comment quite literally: "Do you really like my hat, Cousin Rochelle? I'm glad. I trimmed it myself, you know."

In the end, the relatives had accepted her, more or less. They made allowances. In the first place, she was an orphan; her parents had been killed in a car accident when she was only eighteen. In the second, she came from a small town in the Midwest. Her parents' death left her the only Jew in the entire county. Until she met and married Sidney Waxman, she had never heard of, much less prepared, mandel bread or kashe varnishkes—a state of cultural deprivation which, her in-laws felt, explained much.

Mrs. Waxman sympathized with her daughter's plans to move to New York, live in Greenwich Village, and "write." Indeed, she had fueled her daughter's fantasies for years, with wistful, admiring references to Isadora Duncan and Edna St. Vincent Millay, two women who knew how to live boldly and with flair. Their commitment to Art, she had intimated, excused them from living conventional lives. Neither lady could be expected to end up frying tomatoes or wringing out clothes in a Baltimore rowhouse, surrounded by cranky, incontinent children. Mrs. Waxman spoke feelingly of "the Village," a place she had never visited, but had read much about in both its pre- and post-World War I incarnations. Now, on the brink of Susan's moving there, she dropped thrilling hints of sidewalk cafes and coffeehouses, of wine and poetry, of dark, intense young men. "You must write and tell me everything!" she added.

With Susan's father, Mrs. Waxman chose another tack. Mr. Waxman did not approve of his daughter's plans; he muttered of subway rape, racial hostility, and "Beatniks" in sodden bars. To him, Susan's mother had sensibly pointed out that Marlene Gross, Susan's former roommate, had been living in Manhattan for a year, without dire consequences. Besides, Susan had worked Saturdays and summers all through college and had saved her money; it was unfair to expect her to look for a permanent job the very month of her graduation. "Young people like to try their wings," she had pointed out. "Think of it as a summer vacation, Sidney. If it doesn't work out, she'll come back home."

Susan had cringed, but recognized this as the voice of strategy. In her hazy way, her mother could be Machiavellian.

Marlene Gross had helped Susan locate a two-room apartment in the East Village. (Neither girl could afford to live across the island, in Millay's former neighborhood.) Housed in a red-brick tenement whose walls smelled of Pine-Sol, garlic, and Spanish coffee, it consisted of a bedroom, a kitchen, a bathtub stuck in a trunk-shaped alcove, and a toilet crammed in a closet. A police lock guarded the door, and gates embraced the windows, which looked down into the street where Hispanic men played dominoes all night. Susan loved the place. It was totally unlike anything in Baltimore.

Marlene, who'd been an earnest A-student and secretary of the Class of '66, had changed during her year in Manhattan. She had acquired cool. She spoke offhandedly of the war in Vietnam, marijuana, and Judy Collins concerts in Central Park. She wore new clothes: miniskirts, embroidered peasant blouses, long flowing dresses from Fred Leighton's. Her earring collection was superb; she swung and sparkled when she walked. She worked part-time as a receptionist for a health-food distributor, volunteered part-time to stuff envelopes for a peace organization, and "hung out" the rest of the time. She introduced Susan to the scene.

Admiringly, Susan followed her friend to parties, to "demos," to hip bars like St. Adrian's on Broadway, where it was all right to let strange men pick you up. At first, Susan was surprised. Just eighteen months before, in their dormitory room, Marlene—a drabber, short-haired Marlene—had agreed with Susan and Debbie, their third roommate, that you must never, under any circumstances, give a strange man your phone number. "At the very least," Marlene had said then, solemnly, "you'll lose your self-respect."

In New York, none of these rules seemed to apply. In the bars and coffeehouses, the bearded, book-carrying young men would sit next to Marlene and ask what she "did." "Oh, whatever I feel like," she would respond, with an enticing bounce of earrings, or, "What do *you* think I do?" or, Susan's favorite, "I don't *do*, I just *am*!" All of these seemed to be the right answers; the men would say "Outasight!" and move closer. Susan would look down into her glass of white wine and try not to be too obviously impressed.

Soon Susan was meeting men too. Friends of Marlene's. Her ex-boyfriends. Friends of her ex-boyfriends. Some were artists and some were "political"; many were Jewish. It was easy, and even agreeable, to go home with them, or let them come home with her. The sex was pleasant, never painful, never overly passionate. (Susan's first and only lover back home, a Greek Orthodox engineering student, had been far more difficult and disappointing.) The best part was afterward, when they left. Susan would write highly selective descriptions of these encounters in letters to her mother: "I met a new man tonight, Henry Katz. He has a red beard and makes collages out of hubcaps and wires he finds in the street. He's having a one-man show next month," or "Bernard is a conscientious objector. He's handsome and has suffered terribly for his beliefs. You would like him."

To Marlene, Susan found herself giving accounts of a different type. Her former roommate loved to meet for long confessional breakfasts at Ratner's on Second Avenue. "So, how was Peter?" she'd ask, eagerly buttering an onion roll. "Face it, sexual repression sucks. Tell me everything." At first, to oblige, Susan exaggerated, or invented, details.

But, as the summer wore on, she began to find Marlene irritating, and the unkempt young men tiresome. More and more frequently, when one of them called with another invitation, Susan would make her excuses: "I'm sorry, but I have to work on my *writing* tonight."

Then she would sit at her formica table and change words around in the same sentence. All through college, she'd received A's in Creative Writing; she'd composed whole stories on buses, in laundromats, in the student lounge with the jukebox playing. But her apartment daunted her. Its very bareness challenged her will to create. She could feel her personality draining off into the walls, the floors, evaporating through the window gates, so that she felt as blank as a clean page in her notebook. Or, she'd become too aware of herself, not as creator but as character. She was a "young girl," a "would-be writer," sitting in a secondhand chair at a used table in a tenement apartment in the "hip" East Village, trying to write. This picture of herself squatted firmly in the center of her mind, like mud in a gutter; no other images or impulses could work their through. She seriously considered returning to Baltimore. Then she discovered the Cafe Endgame.

Located in a basement across from Tompkins Square Park, it was a relic of another generation: an ill-lit room, with mismatched tables and chairs, and patrons well into their thirties, and even forties. Dress and manners were considerably less complicated here than in the bars and coffeehouses across town. People wore faded denims, sagging sweaters, and army-surplus jackets. They didn't say much to each other.

At first, Susan had hesitated before entering. It seemed a foreign country, whose language and folkways she did not know; she could make an embarrassing, or dangerous, mistake. But she did go in, trying not to stare at the chess players in the front window, the two cats asleep on a table, the pile of record albums next to the cash register, the pink baby in a papoose-sack, dangling from a hook meant for coats. A thin, dark woman took her order. "We got white bean soup today. Gretta's back," she announced, cryptically. "Want some?" Susan nodded. The soup turned out to be very good. Soon she was going there every day.

The cafe was asocial, yet oddly homey. It was like a family whose members leave each other alone. You could sit there for five minutes or five hours, order a cup of coffee or an entire meal. Susan found it soothing. Nothing was expected of her.

She became friendly with Ruth, the waitress and mother of the dangling baby. Ruth sometimes passed on gossip about the other customers. Susan learned that the jaunty, ropey-necked little man at the corner table was Pete Hansen, the painter, who was somehow connected with the New York School. (Her lover Henry had despised his work.) His untidy, red-haired woman companion was Maggie Murphy, the poet. Her book had caused an explosion in the neighborhood ten years before. She always wore dungarees, a soiled peasant blouse, and a disdainful expression. Sometimes she, and other poets, gave readings of their work at the cafe at night. "You ought to come back here some evening," Ruth said. "It's, like, a livelier scene."

Susan preferred the daytime when the room was dim and quiet, its inhabitants immersed in their various, discrete activities, like dancers in an underwater ballet. She drank coffee, played with the cats, and learned how to operate the quirky record player. With her favorite John Coltrane album as background music, she quickly filled two notebooks with ideas for stories, character sketches, and first paragraphs. She read novel after novel, buying them cheaply in a secondhand bookstore. After all, she reasoned, she couldn't expect to learn technique if she didn't look at other people's work. "I'm getting a lot accomplished here," she wrote to her mother. "The Cafe Endgame is wonderful. Right now I'm sitting across from a famous artist and a famous poet. They've lived together for years. You would love this place."

Susan often fantasized about visiting Cafe Endgame with her mother. It was a place where you *could* bring a mother, as you couldn't bring her to Marlene's favorite West Village coffeehouse. Mrs. Waxman would be thrilled by the chess players, the cats, the music, and the people. She would admire Ruth's baby and Gretta's white bean soup.

Maybe, over coffee, she and Susan would talk. Their unacknowledged conspiracy could at last take shape in words. Her mother would tell Susan what it was like to be a Jew in a small Christian town, or a young woman on her own at eighteen. She would reveal her personality in a way she could never do at home. Freed from the monitory presence of her husband and his many relatives, she might disclose some new information, something Susan needed to know about women, men, art, or the essential business of life.

Then it happened. "How would you like a houseguest?" Mrs. Waxman wrote. "Your ancient mother would love to come to New York for a day or two. I'm dying to see all the exciting sights!" Susan responded with an exuberant letter and an itinerary: the pottery shop, the tiny French restaurant, the good bookstore on St. Mark's Place, the park, and, of course, the Cafe Endgame.

Three days later, Susan's phone rang. Her mother's voice sounded tremulous and distant. "Lovey, there's been a change in plans. It's your father. He's going to drive us to New York so we can visit his cousin in Port Jefferson the next day. He hasn't seen Herbie in years."

At first, Susan said nothing at all. "Does he have to come?" she asked finally, in a small voice.

"Oh, lovey—you know how hard your father works!"

"But I wanted to see *you*. I wanted to show you—"

"Don't worry. I won't cramp your style!" Mr. Waxman's voice broke in. He had been there all the time, Susan realized, listening on the extension. "You girls just go ahead and do whatever you want. Just pretend I'm not there."

A week later, Susan met her parents at the Midtown Motor Court. She had dressed carefully for the occasion, in a green striped minidress and large plastic earrings. Her father stared disapprovingly at this outfit. Her mother exclaimed, "Oh, darling, you've lost weight!"

When Susan mentioned the pottery store and the French restaurant, her father grunted. "Lovey, your father wants to go to Howard Johnson's," Mrs. Waxman said, as if in interpretation.

The visit was turning out badly. After lunch at Howard Johnson's, the Waxmans drove down to Susan's apartment. Both parents were shocked by its starkness. "This is terrible!" Mr. Waxman sounded seriously upset. "Why didn't you tell me you lived like this? I could have brought you some *chatchkes* from the store. You know, little personal touches."

"Daddy's right, dear," Mrs. Waxman agreed. "This isn't *you*."

"But I came to write, not to decorate an apartment. I'm not here much anyway. Let me show you the place where I write, the place I told you about. It's around the corner."

"Okay, let's get out of this dump at least," Mr. Waxman agreed, giving Susan's apartment one last, baleful glance.

Turning the corner, Susan felt more hopeful. For one thing, it was a fine, green summer day; in Tompkins Square Park, children were tossing frisbees, and old men and women on benches were gossiping in various languages. In the window of Cafe Endgame, the chess players sat hunched in concentration. The door opened and the nautical-looking artist came out.

For the first time, he looked directly at Susan. "Hi, kid," he said. He took in her parents behind her and gave her a nod before disappearing into the park. It was almost a wink. Susan glowed.

"That's Pete Hansen," she said, mostly to her mother. "The painter I wrote you about." She stepped down into the areaway and began to push open the door. Her mother was right behind her.

"No! I'm not going in there! Not on your life!" Susan's father was standing at the top of the steps, his feet planted firmly apart, like a balky bulldog's. "That man looks like a drug addict."

Susan couldn't believe this was happening. She stood awkwardly holding the door open. Her mother paused uncertainly on the stairs.

"Who comes here anyway?" Mr. Waxman asked, loudly. "Drug addicts and prostitutes!" he answered himself. "Whores and bums!"

The chess players looked up from their game. One giggled and the other guffawed. Susan wanted to die.

"Sidney, if Susan's friends—"

"Don't tell me about this place! I know all about it. Look, Julia, you can go in if you want, but not me. I'm not crazy!" Mr. Waxman turned and marched around the corner, in the direction of his car. His shoulders were stiff with indignation.

Susan had a wonderful thought. Maybe her mother would ignore her father's rantings, and they'd go in and drink coffee together, just as she'd planned. But Mrs. Waxman apologetically climbed back to the sidewalk.

"I'm sorry, lovey, but we have to find your father. You know how he is."

The rest of the visit was dreadful. They ate dinner at a very expensive restaurant on the Upper East Side. No one spoke much. Once, when Mrs. Waxman was in the ladies' room, Susan's father glared at his daughter, grunted, and declared, "You're killing your mother!" Susan looked down at her uneaten lamb chop. She said nothing.

As soon as she could, Susan left her parents at their motel. "I'll call you tomorrow, lovey," Mrs. Waxman said. Mr. Waxman gave her five dollars for a cab. Defiantly, she took the subway.

But she knew she couldn't go back to her apartment. Never had it seemed less inviting. She headed for the Cafe Endgame.

It was different, at night. Every table was crammed. The crowd was younger than usual, and better dressed. The chess players and red-haired poet were still there, but they seemd out of place, odd bits of flotsam caught in the waves of laughing young people in miniskirts and paisley ties.

A strange, supercilious man conducted Susan to a table. "Only one?" he made a face. "You'll have to share."

"I'll have a bowl of white bean soup," Susan sank into a chair.

"Kitchen's closed."

"Well, a cup of coffee, then."

"What kind?"

"What do you mean?"

"Espresso? Cappuccino? Cafe au lait?" He sounded annoyed.

"Oh. Cappuccino." Susan was disconcerted. She'd never had to make such a choice at the Cafe Endgame before. She'd always been served plain American coffee in a chipped white mug.

Instead of the record player, a rock group was performing on an improvised stage. Its members wore costumes modelled on Tenniel's drawings for *Alice in Wonderland.* The lead singer was Alice, the two guitarists were the Mad Hatter and the White Rabbit, and the drummer was the Dormouse. Susan thought they were awful. She wanted to leave.

"Hey, don't I know you from somewhere?"

For the first time, Susan realized that she was sharing her table with a man: a short, compact, vaguely handsome young man with a thick moustache.

"I've seen you around," he said, "with that Marlene Gross."

"You know Marlene?"

"Yeah, I know her. She's a busy chick. She's a chick with problems. I could tell her things, you know, about herself."

"You could?" Susan was intrigued. She wondered if she could ask him what he thought Marlene's problems were. Before she was able to say anything, her companion produced a Baggie full of marijuana and some rolling papers. To Susan's astonishment, he proceeded to roll a joint right there on the table. Her friends—Marlene's friends—all "smoked," of course, but not quite so publicly.

"Have some," the man passed the joint, rolled and lit, to Susan. "Good dope. Name's Bob, by the way. Bob Cantor."

Susan didn't care much for grass. It was supposed to make you passionate and creative. It usually made her hungry and nervous. Yet she found herself accepting. The waiter appeared with her coffee. Soon both coffee and joint were consumed.

"I know where there's some even better stuff," Bob said, coyly. "In my room."

Bob's apartment was filled with strangely old-fashioned mahogany furniture. There were no curtains on his windows. He brought out a sock filled with more grass, and the rolling and lighting-up rituals were repeated. Susan wished they'd get to the next stage. After her harrowing day, she wanted to be held, cuddled, made love to.

It seemed like hours before they were undressed and pleasantly tangled in the big bed. "Hey, babe, I like your bod!" Bob exclaimed. He kissed her nipples. She allowed herself to grow mildly excited. He held her and rubbed up and down against her body. She rubbed back.

More time passed. Bob's rubbings grew less pleasant, more impatient. Their skins became hotter, sweaty and slippery. Their flesh stuck together in places, then pulled apart with little sucking noises. Susan thought of a bandage being torn off a skinned knee.

The mild haze of sexual interest evaporated. They became two strange people rubbing away at each other in a hot room for no particular reason. His moustache brushed across her mouth. It tasted like a clump of damp weeds.

She reached down and felt for his penis. It was not hard. She didn't know what to do. None of her other lovers had ever taken this long to complete what they'd started.

Abruptly, Bob sat up. "Let's try again later." Susan agreed, relieved. They smoked another joint.

But when they tried later, the results were the same. Susan grew distraught. "What can I do?" she asked.

"Like, use your imagination, babe."

But her imagination was of no use; her mind was full of smoke. Her other men had apparently possessed far simpler sexual machinery; or perhaps they were more attracted to her. She felt a failure. All of her exertions in the sexual revolution had not prepared her for this moment.

Gingerly, she took Bob's penis in her hand. To her dismay, it shrank down to an even smaller size. What *was* she doing wrong? She stroked it gently. That didn't help.

Turning around on the moist bed, she eyed it closely. It looked like a squat parsnip root. Her father's Aunt Rose had showed her how to select parsnips for soup. "Firm, not limp, that's the secret," she had declared, poking each one with an experienced finger.

Thinking of Aunt Rose reminded Susan that her parents were still in the city. She grew tight with fear. What if they had, somehow, come back to the East Village to look for her? What if they were looking for her right now? Afraid to glance in the direction of Bob's naked window, she tried to concentrate on his problematical private parts. But she kept hearing her parents' voices: "Oh, lovey, we *trusted* you," her mother wailed. "Whore! Bum! Drug addict!" her father bellowed in despair—or was it triumph?

"Look, Bob, I've got to go now," Susan slid out of bed and rummaged for her clothes on the floor. "My parents are in town and they're going to call me at twelve-thirty. I've got to be home or they'll have a fit."

"Yeah, parents are a drag," Bob agreed, evenly. His tone revealed nothing—not anger, not disappointment.

"I'm sorry," said Susan, backing out the door. She tried not to think of him lying there, alone and frustrated. She hoped he could console himself with a joint.

Her phone was indeed ringing as she unlocked the door. It was her mother. "Darling, where have you been? Your father is sick. As soon as you left, he started throwing up."

"I'm sorry," Susan said, for the second time in fifteen minutes.

"You know Daddy. Everything affects his stomach. A motel doctor saw him. He thinks he'll be well enough to travel tomorrow, so I'll drive him home. We'll skip the visit to Herbie."

"You're saying goodbye?"

"Yes, dear. I'll write you."

When she hung up, Susan sat holding the receiver for a long time.

The next week was painfully empty. Susan couldn't go back to the Cafe Endgame; she was afraid she might see Bob there. She didn't want to call Marlene or any of her short-term lovers. She didn't write to her mother. She didn't feel like writing anything.

The city itself was inert. A hot metal lid of a sky seemed clamped on the simmering buildings and streets. Susan walked for hours. She found it hard to talk to anyone. She wore the same clothes day after day. In a way, the city had turned into her apartment; she rattled around in it blindly, unable to summon the energy or personality necessary to impose on its vastness. One afternoon, she wandered into a cramped luncheonette. The man behind the counter looked like her father. "All the garbage comes in here," he said, to no one in particular. Susan walked out.

Finally, a letter from her mother arrived. After pages of news about relatives, Mrs. Waxman remarked: "Daddy and I are so glad we visited our girl in her New York apartment. The East Village seems interesting and exciting. The Cafe Endgame was a quaint, romantic-looking old place. I'm glad you showed it to us."

Susan was not prepared for the rage she felt. "Liar! Hypocrite!" she screamed, then tore the letter in several pieces and flushed them down the toilet. Immediately, she felt guilty. She knew she would have to go out. She couldn't stay in the apartment, the scene of her outburst of violence.

For hours, she walked. She walked down the Bowery through the old Lower East Side, through Chinatown and the Wall Street area. All of these neighborhoods, like food at a dull cafeteria, seemed insipid and oddly similar. She trudged up Broadway and trailed around the West Village. She found the narrow house where Edna St. Vincent Millay had lived with her husband.

When she returned to the East Village, it was dinnertime. But she didn't feel like eating. At the secondhand bookshop, she picked up novel after novel. She turned to a famous sad ending, and wondered if it would make her cry. Then she felt someone staring at her.

"Hey, babe." It was Bob Cantor. Incredibly, he seemed friendly. "How you doin'? Good to see you. Go to the End much lately?"

It took her a moment to realize he meant the Cafe Endgame.

"No, not since the night I—met you there."

"Oh, right. Nice night. Real groovy dope. Guess what, I got some more."

Susan couldn't think of a response. "Good," she said finally.

"Hey, I'll be at the End tonight. Good group there—in from LA. Maybe I'll see you later. We could, you know, get together."

"Maybe," Susan managed to say. "Got to go now."

Walking home, Susan kept replaying this encounter in her mind. She simply couldn't fit Bob's words to the actions—or non-actions—of their evening together. Had he been trying to save face, or spare her embarrassment? Why had he suggested another meeting? Did he want to make up for their failed one-night stand? Or, had he actually *had* a nice night? It was possible. After all, Susan decided, it takes very little to make some people happy. This thought was comforting.

As she turned into First Avenue, the world seemed much less predictable than she'd realized. The sheer number of choices, or responses, was dizzying. Any strategy for navigating through such a world—any strategy that worked—seemed impressive, if not always adequate.

Susan felt hungry. She stopped at the Jewish bakery on East 9th Street. The owner was elderly and flirtatious.

"Hey, girlie, I'll bet you're new in town. How do you like the Big Apple?"

"I like it." It was true. New York seemed promising once more, a place she could live in.

"What do you do here, dolly?"

"I don't *do*, I just *am*," Marlene's reply spilled out, surprising Susan. She giggled. The old man stared. Then he laughed. For a minute, they laughed together.

When Susan arrived home with her cheesecake, she found that he had given her over half-a-pound, and only charged her for a quarter.

Tiger on Third Avenue

BY IRVING STETTNER

HERE IS A STORY I PICKED UP ONLY YESTERDAY. When I visited my friend Eddie Vincent in his music shop on lower 3rd Avenue, East Side, New York City, U.S.A. of the Cockeyed Beautiful Cosmos incorporated with wonders and blunders, love, anguish, flashing sunlight and laughter.

But wait—before visiting Eddie I first dropped in on pal Morris Feinstein, the pharmacist in the drug store down the block.

For the last ten years now, a morning come around when I wake up broke, I've often gone down to see Maurey, and he has yet to let me down.

If I've been lucky, I bring along the latest issue of some magazine—usually oddball, small press or underground—which has published a poem of mine and sent me a contributor's copy.

Soon as I walk in the door—"Look who's here," Maurey cries out blithely, "Downtown Shakespeare! Hi ya, Irv!" He is behind the oily mahogany counter as usual, his big brown frog eyes twinkling brightly through thick horn-rimmed glasses, his thin lips smiling, his unruly shock of black hair tossing dandruff down onto the shoulders of the same frayed brown striped suit that I've seen him wear for the past ten years.

"What, you've been inspired so quickly?" he exclaims. "You were just here last week! I knew I should never have sold you those goof balls!"

"No, it was a month ago, Maurey." And he never sold me any dope; simply joking, Maurey, as always, since he can't help it, since he happens to be a natural-born, truly great comedian.

"What's it this time?" he asks, glancing at the periodical in my hand.

"*Xanadu*, a review from Arizona."

"Hm, what's that, a new type of tropical fruit? Never mind—how much?"

"Three bucks."

"*Three?*" Maurey repeats faintly, and coughs harshly a few times... "Do you have a glass of water in your pocket, any chance?"

"No!"

"Okay." And handing me three singles: "Oh well, I'm sure your poem is a masterpiece. But when the hell are you going to be famous, Irv? that's what I want to know! It's about time, don't you think? Gad, this must be the 20th mag or book that I've bought from you! Did you take my advice—what I told you the last time?"

"No... what was it anyhow?"

"I forget myself." There is a customer in the store, waiting for a prescription: an elderly bald, stocky Polish guy leaning on an oak cane; with serious mien and multi-furrowed brow, as if any minute he was going to fall straight into his grave.

Still Maurey lets me follow him into the small back room, where he grinds and mixes his chemicals, and keeps up a running conversation: "What to do with all your books... You know what? Pretty soon I'll have to buy a new bookcase!"

"How did you like the last one?"

"Never had a chance to read it. I gave it to my daughter; she's crazy about your work, believe it or not."

"She is? I'd like to meet her someday."

"Oh, would you now? Not a chance! Do I need a broke poet for a son-in-law? Like a *lock in kop*" (hole in the head—Yiddish).

"Anyway Maurey," I announce, taking out my pen, "I'm going to sign this one for you."

"How-about-that. Does it mean the mag is worth more?"

"Sure, it always is. Though come to think of it—maybe *less*!"

"Oh well, another collector's item."

"Thanks, Maurey."

"Yes, I have all your books at home, and they're all collecting dust."

"Ha-ha! That's what I like about coming in here."

"What—the three bucks?"

"Eh—yes. Still it never fails: you always make me laugh!"

"Irv, I'm only here to fill prescriptions."

"That's just what I mean! As Rabelais once said: 'For all your ills I give you laughter.' "

"*Rabelais*?"

"Yes, François Rabelais: didn't you ever hear of him?"

"Sure, he was in here yesterday."

See what I mean? Going out the door, I'm practically in convulsions with laughter. Hell, I reflect, I should be paying this guy Maurey—just to be allowed to visit him!

I walked back down St. Marks Place, one block in order to check my mailbox. With the perennial glint of hope that I'll find the letter I'm always waiting subliminally for. One from big Doubleday, or Harcourt, Brace & Jovanovich publishers: *Dear Mr. Stettner: Please come immediately to our office, as we have a contract ready for you to sign. We feel simply compelled to print a deluxe edition of your Collected Works, one on imported Suzuki rice paper, with color illustrations by French artist Maurice de Bontemps...* In other words I'm always ready for a miracle, like even finding a letter from the ghost of Rita Hayworth, Van Gogh or Mihály Zichy. Actually there *are* three letters in the mailbox: One, from a feminist periodical in Chicago with enclosed payment in check for a poem, $3.50. Two, a Gas & Electric bill for $89.53. Three, a letter from my nephew Stanley who is attending University of California, on a fellowship to do research work; he wants to thank me for the little book of poems that I sent him, he writes, and informs me that his career as a psycho-neurologist is going great guns: this week he will start vivisection on a few baby field rabbits...

Also in the mailbox—or tucked halfway into its steel slot so I'll be sure to notice it—is a small folded note from my girlfriend Anita: "*Dear Irving, How can you speak about marriage—when you can't even support yourself! You must be nuts! etc.*"

I walk back up the street. "Hi'ya' doing, Irv!" cries a voice cheerily, and I'm face to face with Carilyn.

"Oh, I could do better, I could do worse," I reply, giving her a real Zen response, forthright and gratuitous. Carilyn, a dipsy blonde from the neighborhood with mammoth cow breasts whom every time I run into raps me right down to the ground, a half-hour gab session. All about her interest in the theatre, how badly she wants to be an actress; and same which I've been hearing for three years now. Meanwhile no results, since Carilyn has failed to take even the first step toward her big dream. Or is it isn't acting, she talks endlessly about Macrobiotics, Tai-Chi, the American Indian situation, and the best species of marijuana floating around. However, this time I quickly brush her off.

It is a hot, sweltering summer day, the air like melted butter. A few steps more and I run into Three-Finger Louis, who is stumbling along with an open beer quart in one hand. He stops me, and bums a cigarette. Louis, an ex-junkie who is trying to kick the cocaine habit with methadone—and alcohol.

On the corner of 2nd Avenue, it's so hot my shirt is already drenched with sweat. Suddenly I feel quirky and faint, my head spins dizzily around . . . like a merry-go-round suddenly going full speed, out of whack. A severe case of sun-stroke—or Rimbaudian hallucination? Anyway just as the red light turns to green, I hear the magic little *click* in the metal box attached to the corner lamp-post, I feel a big ache in my head as if it's bursting open, and out from my fore-head pops a large bloodshot eyeball. I see it shoot straight into the air four feet, then fall to the sidewalk where in two seconds flat it becomes a bright yellow billiard ball which bounces and rolls gingerly forward, over the curb and into the heavy traffic, beneath the wheels of the passing cars . . .

Then glancing around, I see a large crowd assembled in front of the Savings bank. They are all down on the knees bowing their heads in humble salaams, fervently, rapidly waving their arms up and down, again and again, and all in the direction of the bank's front revolving door. But at that particular spot, sud-denly—now stands a fat, ten foot high chocolate-frosted donut! The crowd cries out in delight "Alleluia!" Meanwhile I look at the donut's hole, its invisible center, look and stare long and hard till, lo and behold! I see the gold face of the Buddha, his bright shining visage and enigmatic smile . . .

Three Puerto Rican kids on skateboards suddenly whiz up the street, onto the scene. They hold upright in their hands a large red banner, with printed on it in big black letters: "VIVA ZAPATA! HURRAH FOR NOTHING! DEATH TO THE DEATH EATERS! SHIT, GET MY SOUL OFF THE OPERATING TABLE!"

Am I dreaming, or what? I blink my eyes hard, a few times; perhaps it is all a mirage—induced by the heat? Whatever, a police car suddenly speeding up 2nd Avenue with its siren howling, snaps me out of it. And there I am, back on the corner standing in front of the Manufacturers Hanover Trust Bank, looking at its bright marble exterior, its sparkling white, immaculate, cold, vacuous, beautyless, minus a spark of imagination, nondescript-as-shit facade.

Then a block west to 3rd Avenue, where I drop in on my pal Eddie Vincent, owner of the Singing Rainbow Music Shop.

My luck here, dubious; all depends whether or not Eddie, a guitar player, is in the mood to have a jam session with a couple of his musician friends. If so then there'll be one right in the middle of the store, and the Singing Rainbow will be closed for the rest of the day. Hell with business! True, if I knock on the door he'll let me in, regardless, to hear their playing. Still I'm not likely to interrupt it; and I usually get so carried away, turned-on by their music—especially if it's far-our—I forget altogether why I have come to visit Eddie, viz., to sell him a mag, or borrow a five spot perhaps.

But I'm in luck, today the shop is open. Eddie—or "Tiger" as his friends call him—Vincent may seem innocuous, what with his frail 5'5" frame, rimless glasses, hair slightly grey and habitual gentle, congenial smile. But he is a firebrand, full of piss and vinegar, believe me.

As I walk through the door, a customer steps abruptly in front of me. He is a tall young dude wearing a hat and tie, decorously dressed, carrying a leather briefcase.

He speaks in a low, suave voice, like some university professor. "Do you have any electric Gibson guitars?"

"Sure," replies Eddie.

"Can I look at one?"

"That depends: do you have any money?"

"Well, eh—not on me."

"Then go get some, and I'll let you look at the guitar."

"What? But—"

"Listen, mister, why waste your time and mine? *See you later, pal!*"

"Hi ya, poet!" Eddie greets me. "Where the hell have you been? I know—flush; you only come around when you're broke, you fuck. Never mind. But wait—don't move an inch." He hands me a ten dollar bill. "Now truck on down to the Deli on 14th Street and buy us two corned beef sandwiches. Make mine lean, lettuce and mustard, and get a couple of large Schaefers. We're going to celebrate, b'Jesus!"

Eddie "Tiger" Vincent is one of the top Hawaiian guitar players in the country. A few years ago, turning fifty and tired of the travelling life of a musician, he opened the Singing Rainbow. He lives with his wife Helen, and their little twelve inch chihuahua, Koochie, in a small but neat pad over on East 10th Street. Eddie was in the Korean War, a combat engineer attached to the Marines. Toward the end of it he was badly wounded, which included the loss of one eye. Still I wouldn't mess with Eddie Vincent, no sir-ee. There was a guy who did once, tried to hold up Eddie in the street; and twice his size too, but I know for a fact that five seconds later he was lying stretched out on the pavement, stone cold. Eddie is also an ace exponent of karate, a skill he picked up in the Marines.

I'm back with the sandwiches and beer. We dig in, a few bites and Eddie spins away: "Yes, my daughter Ruth finally got hitched. And it would never have happened—if not for me!

"It's this way. Ever since Ruth was sixteen she went steady with only one guy, name of Ernie. They met in high school, and just hit it off together. Even when they both graduated, and Ernie went on to college and law school, and Ruth became a secretary, they went right on seeing one another. Ernie always coming around to the house to take Ruth out, to dinner or a movie, a few times a week. I thought for sure they would get spliced, sooner or later.

"But then come the day Ernie graduated from law school, and presto, we never saw him again. And neither did Ruth. Would you believe it? All we knew was that he had returned to Omaha, Nebraska, where his folks lived and went to work in his father's meat packing plant.

"My wife Helen was freaked-out, completely puzzled by it. But I wasn't. Yes, I knew what had happened. I even spoke to Ruth, asked her straight out about it; and she said, yes, it was true. What was? She had never given Ernie any sex, that's what. And come graduation day—well, the guy thought he was finally entitled to some. And could you blame him? Christ, he had been going with her for ten years!

"Well, you know women. She wanted Ernie to marry her first, a ring on her finger, so on. And Ruth—she's just like her mother, the same disposition... Why, do you know what my wife calls me sometimes?—*a sex maniac*! Beat that, will ya! Oh, my wife, I'm about ready to give up on her. I remember when I first met her 25 years ago, she was just off that truck farm in Ohio, which she had been working on since she was twelve years old. Working from dawn till night, all she knew was drudgery. Why I married her perhaps? Yes, I felt sorry for her, and tried to make her happy... But has anything ever worked out? No! Like two years ago, when I bought that little house out in Long Island. Just not for her, she said, no. So we had to move right back to New York City. She is always moping, that's the trouble. Feeling sorry for herself, always thinking of the past... Though how many times have I told her: forget the past, will ya'! The past is gone and over with, it took a shit and died a long, long time ago!

"Yes, Ruth is just like her mother—stubborn. How many times have I told the kid: Listen, hell, if you like a guy, sleep with him. Go right ahead! Gad, fucking—there's nothing wrong with it. Hasn't it been going on for 5000 years? And everybody does it: the ice man, the TV repair man, his wife Gertie, Shmertie, the baker, the shoemaker—everybody fucks. And can you blame them? It's part of human nature!

"No, she wouldn't listen. So it was good-bye Ernie. Then my daughter starts going after other guys: first a saxophone player, than a Yale student, a car salesman, a Hindu for a couple of weeks, so, a few other shmucks. But none of them ever last long. Then she decides what she really needs is her own place. So she moves out to Brooklyn, finds a small apartment in Park Slope.

"Now and then she visits us; sits and talks, and often drops Ernie's name. So I know what's up, whom she's thinking about... and that she's unhappy.

"So a month ago, finally one morning I walk over to the phone, ask Information and get Ernie's number in Omaha. I call him, yes.

"'Hello?' Ernie answers, at the other end of the line. 'Oh, it's you, Dad (way he always addressed me.)'

"'Ernie, I have something to speak to you about. Maybe I should have written you a letter—but when it comes to writing—well, you know how I am. Anyway Ernie, tell me: why did you and Ruth break up?'

"'Well, Dad, eh—'

"'Kid, I *know* why. You don't have to tell me.'

"'You do?'

"'Sure. Only things have changed, Ernie. You still stand a good chance... savvy what I'm trying to say?'

"'Yes.'

"'Alright, I'll give you her address. But first, Ernie, tell me: do you love her—for *real*, I mean?'

"'Yes, Dad!'

"'Okay, then here it is: 189 Carroll Street, Apartment 4B, and in Brooklyn, as I said. Have it? Good—now go get her, son!' And I hung up.

"That was on a Friday. I knew it would take him about a day to come to New York. So Sunday morning I stayed in, hung around the apartment. And come 10 o'clock, with my wife Helen in the living room watching some loony TV show, suddenly the phone rang. And it was Ruth, just as I figured.

"'Guess what, Pa,' she said over it. 'Ernie is back. He's here now in my place.'

"'Is that right?' I remarked, real nonchalant.

"'Yes, Pa, can we come around and visit you?'

"'No, Ruth.'

"'*What?*'

"'No,' I repeated. 'Now listen, Ruth; this is Eddie your father speaking, right? And have I ever steered you wrong, gal?'

"'No, Pa.'

"'Then will you listen to me now?'

"'Yes.'

"'Okay, then you do just as I say. Ernie is there, right? Okay, you go to the front door, lock it and then—*fuck him to death!*' And I hung up.

"Helen heard it all, and started to yell blue murder, nash'. But I quickly shut her up, and said: 'If we had any sense we'd be in the bedroom right now, doing the same thing!'

"Then a couple of days went by without a word from Brooklyn. My wife wanted to visit them, Ruth and Ernie. 'Nix,' I said, 'Nothing doing! We just sit still and leave them alone awhile.'

"A week later, Ruth finally phoned me. She was in the City Hall building, downtown. 'Pa,' she said, all excited, 'Ernie and I just got married!'

"The next evening, Ruth, Ernie, me and the missus all went to Luchow's for a big dinner. A T-bone steak, red and white wine, the works. And middle of it, do you know what my daughter said to me? Well, she came over and whispered in my ear: 'Thanks, Pa. And let me tell you: gee, Ernie in bed—he's terrific!"

"Okay, Irv, so now you have it. How's that for a story? Go home and knock it off on your typewriter. Good as any poem you ever wrote, isn't it? Wait—you're looking skinny as hell these days. Better first go back to the Deli, and buy us two more corned beef sandwiches. And make it a couple of coffees this time. How do I like mine? With two sugars, and light: remember, light—*without* milk. Ha-ha!"

Can I Get You Something?

BY MAX BLAGG

YOU WANNIT? YOU WANNIT? OH I BET YOU DO wanna match? Wanna Match Factor cream in your coffee
wanna lipstick on your collar loose joints
smack? acid? cocaine?
Ups, downs, insides and outsides starboards and floorboards
wanna floor it? wanna bury the needle on this landshark
wanna step on the gas wanna crash and burn
wanna see the car burn
wanna picture of my car burning?
wanna buy some pictures wanna see the movie?
wanna buy the out-takes? Want some take out?
Want some chow fun honey wanna chow down
wanna get some?
Then you better get it from me 'cos I know he ain't giving you none
ah that's not nice you wanna drink?

wanna beer wanna warm beer turn left at Schaefer City
hey not so fast there buddy you wanna ticket?
Oh you wanna buy a ticket? wanna ticket to ride
wanna slide down a razor blade?
Wanna go a couple of rounds think you're a tough guy?
Why don't you do yourself a favor and watch through the keyhole
while I go a couple of rounds with your wife?
Is that what you want? Wanna get laid?
wanna get paid for your work?
Sorry, I'm sorry, you can't have it.
You can't afford it.
Hey, hey, wanna dance wanna tango, piranha two step
wanna rip it up and ball tonight?
Do you wanna get down wanna get down
wanna get up off the ground
you want a policeman wanna call the cops?
Dial 911 and wait two hours.
Do you know what you want?
Want the good life full of fun seems to be the ideal?
Of course you do ... that's what you want
I'll bet on it
Wanna bet? wanna bet on it? Wanna bet on a sure thing?
Well bet with your head not over it
'cos you're in this over your head already
you're in this over your head already...
What? You lost your bet again?
Well, you can't afford it then can you?
You can't have it.

● ● ●

Oh well ... wanna watch TV? Wanna see Love Boat?
Wanna fuck the midget on 'Fantasy Island'?
Wanna TV Guide—Want your own personal TV pilot
wanna jet pilot wanna astronaut?
Hey WAIT!
I'm sorry, you can't have it. You can't afford it.
What do you want it for anyway if I give it to you?
What are you gonna do with it when you get it?
Where are you gonna put it?
You don't have the space.
Hey you wanna buy a space? Wanna go co-op?
wanna live downtown where all the lights are bright?
wanna have your own personal space

want some space for that tiny head of yours?
Wanna get rich quick wanna be a star?
Be a doorman, open a store
sell teddybears, french underwear...
Hey! hey you're wanted...you're wanted on the phone
you're wanted by the police the FBI the CIA
Ronald McDonald Billy Graham
and God wants you to be his co-pilot
But you can't you can't afford it
you can't have it.

Now you're in this bar business
Yeah, what do you want? You wanna peenya what?
Sorry the blender's broken and we're fumigating the place tonight
so you'll have to leave.
You wanna what? you wanna booth? No we don't, not for two I'm sorry
hey can't you see I'm busy? Oh yeah? Oh yeah well
I am the manager so get your face out of here!
Hey you! You can't bring that dog in here!
It's dead! I don't care if it was killed by a rabbi
take it out of the bar right now!
Oh yeah? Well talk to my lawyer then if that's what you want
that's what you want isn't it?
Yeah sure he'll be in touch if that's what you want
but you're gonna find out that you can't afford it
you can't afford any of it.

Hey, er listen, wanna woman? wanna blonde? Wanna big woman
a real Rubens, a flatbed hussy built like a truck?
You clown she'll run right over you!
You can't afford it anyway...
Oh you wannit, you wannit,
I know you wannit
But I'm sorry you can't have it
and you'll never get it
because even if you could afford it
there's no way in the world
you could have it.

The Muffins of Sebek

BY ED SANDERS

*As the gluons
bind the neutrons
within the atom's core—
so too Rent Control
binds us to the
Perfect City.*

*O Rent Control!
You are the root,
the bast, the base
of any decent way of life
in a land where
food is abundant!*

Rent Control!

SAM THOMAS SPENT THE MORNING WORKING on his "Hymn to Rent Control." It was difficult searching for fresh images to sustain an ancient concern. It couldn't be just doggerel or the empty shuffle of a bundle of placards dropped resignedly behind the sofa after the demonstration.

But, man, he loved rent control! That most powerful of decencies, the right to live cheaply in good housing even if your country or city is convulsed in spasms of greed and landboomers.

Speaking of rent control, Sam's ebullience began to wane toward noon, as he began to worry about his $51 rent-controlled rent. His normal practice was not to think about it till the 20th, after which it usually was an easy project to raise the cash.

But not this month, when he faced the phenomenon of poverty-within-poverty, a grim condition subsumed within the concept of long term poverty. Sam and his beatnik pals had long ago acquired a tolerance for long term pov—the sudden shut-offs of heat in mid-winter, water pouring from ceilings onto paintings, junkies stealing the few shiny objects from your junk. But there was somehow always a surplus for art. If you could scrounge the rent, then money for food, thrills and art supplies somehow always arrived. But not this month. Sam Thomas was down, busted, without a cent, with no job, no prospect, and without a single friend from whom he could borrow some bread.

The only food he had was a fifty pound bag of oatmeal with which he made his daily banquet of Yum—soy sauce, raw eggs, Hellman's mayonnaise and raw oats glopped together in a wooden bowl. In times of drought he did without the Hellman's and the eggs.

Sam stood up from his desk and began to pace the room, instructing his mind to come up with ten or fifteen instant formulae for cash. He felt the same nervous twinge in the stomach as just before a sit-in at the Atomic Energy Commission. His close friends were similarly afflicted with sudden poverty. Nelson Saite, Miriam Levy, Talbot the Great, Cynthia Pruitt, Louise Adams—dimeless. All were in their respective pads worried, plotting, making lists, consulting the phone numbers of relatives in address books, lining up hockable items on kitchen drainboards, stirring pots of coffee and biting lips.

Not many blocks from where Sam Thomas was pacing his bamboo floor mat, Uncle Thrills was beginning what he railingly described as a "3-day penury whack." Thrills too had the iron hobs of pov in his face and had vowed to remain at home till he'd solved the problem. Home for Thrills was a tiny pad in a decrepit back building that actually leaned to the side so much that it was known on the set as the "leaning pad of Thrill Street." Only by resting against the building to its left did Thrills' back place manage to stand. There were long iron rods impaled through it and into the next building that kept it from wobbling. Its bricks were heavily charred from what must have been a great fire sometime in its 200 year existence. There were zigzags of cracks leading up to marble window plinths through mortar so crumbly that many bricks could be plucked out at will. The place had been an instant slum when speculators had quick-built it in the 18th century on top of the kitchen garden of the house in front, and it was still a slum.

Thrills allowed no one, except an occasional woman, to visit him. He always tried to fling aloft the legend that his apartment was a luxurious citadel of genius, hidden in the slums like the lair of Balzac, a place where he could work the tribulations of his calling. The truth was that he lived in a chaos of loner-hood. Not that Thrills lacked lovers, for he always attracted those surprisingly numerous women who are drawn to wizened, beaten-down and fatally flawed creative types. He was a master at plying the Love-a-Loser Factor, his ravaged and pitted face defying the vicious, stupid world and his hand trying not to shake with oppression as he handed the sheaf of verse to the damozel in the cafe, just minutes after meeting her. In an hour or two they would be quick-stripping by the bed in her apartment.

He always stalled bringing them to his pad, for the Love-a-Loser Factor, strong as it was, usually could not hold up under the horror of encountering Thrills' rooms, which in the fifteen years he'd lived there had never been dusted or swept except for the table where he ate and wrote, and in the sense that the paths from toilet to bed to table to bookcase were broomed by the scuffle of sock and slipper.

Neat stacks of books, newspapers, underwear, socks, notepapers, etc., six feet high or more lined the walls. Now and then one would topple in an ozy-mandian jumble, and if it wedged in an out of the way place it would just lie there for eight or nine years while long gray skuz grew upon it like the tufty remains of an animal long deceased on the forest floor.

In spite of the hispid forest floor of it—I mean, just *walking through* his pad wearing clean clothes and not getting dirty was a big project—Thrills would always emerge in the clean, pressed, perfumed and colorful clothes of a dandy or boulevardier, his bountiful black hair with two wide streaks of white in front like perfectly combed marble curlings, and his shoes as shiny as an oily East Side gutter puddle. There were hints of the struggle here and there in his pad—a box of spotting cloths and the smell of carbon tetrachloride, a suitcase full of 12-year-old shoe polishes, cracked and dried, most with only tiny chunks still wet enough to be used, and a jumble of former shirts, now blotched polish-ing rags.

There was no thought of fophood this afternoon as Thrills sat at his desk in black and white checked flannel pajamas, torn at the crotch, that were down and out in grimesville, man, grimesville. Taped to his typewriter's housing was an odd notation—"3 for 5," which meant he had three days to make the $500 a porn publisher was offering for a completed manuscript. The publisher was one of those who take sadistic pleasure in setting unrealistic deadlines. In this case, if Thrills did not submit it in three days, the deal was off.

"Another Dharma Bum whack," muttered Thrills. He was referring to Jack Kerouac, a friend from long nights at the San Remo bar on MacDougal in the '50s. Thrills had always marveled at Kerouac's ability to click out books quickly. The 1953 *Subterraneans* had been written in three days and the '57 *Dharma Bums* hadn't taken much longer. Thrills knew he could stay awake three straight days before swerving into coma—the problem was to stay creative. As in Kerouac's case, the speed of the key-click was to be augmented by ampheta-mine. A needle was boiling in a pan on the stove. Thrills had also devised a methedrine vaporizer to switch on at crucial times for billowing an energizing though possibly corrosive methedrinous fog on his mucous membranes and lungs.

Thrills always had trouble with his opening sentence. The first 35 words were almost as much of a toil as the 50,000 that followed. This afternoon he was already up to his 47th:

The bat dick slid into the left nostril of the Countess while Count Cornflower stroked its wings with a stalk of celery.

"Owl quim!" he cursed, x-ing it through and searching for another way to begin his tale of interspecies love.

Dr. Whitney held the enema bag in triumph as he walked toward the zebra.

No again.

Her jissom-drenched lips slid across the sea lion's flipper along a trail of chocolate covered ants toward Count Bithecomb's pecker...

"That's it!" he exclaimed, and went forward without a pause into a long and twisted tale of towers, enemas, frottage, celery stalks, oil-dipped corsets and cravings for zebras in castles.

The very moment Uncle Thrills had found his opening sentence, Talbot Jenkins was giving the signal at Andrew Kliver's pad—four raps, a pause, then a single rap. Cynthia Pruitt was at his side, wearing a dress for the first time since the sit-in at the U.N. two months ago. She could only stay a few minutes—she was beginning a job waiting tables at the House of Nothingness and they were making her flash gams as part of the gig.

Kliver opened the door. He was bent over, standing in longsleeved cream-colored long johns and socks, with a stiff white clerical collar around his neck and a five-inch silver cross suspended on his chest from a thin black ribbon. Kliver was a minister in a beatnik Catholic sect called "The Gnostic Rite of Old Glastonbury." His lids were drooping; he'd just shot up. He was holding a kitten in one arm.

Talk about sudden poverty! Both Talbot the Great and Cynthia Pruitt were glum with it. Christmas was just ten days away and Talbot was down to six dol-lars while Cynthia had only a subway token and the Catholic Worker soup line. As tough and revolutionary as their chatter was, there were elements in their attitudes similar to the silent, self-doubting depression of broke Americans at Christmas, the sort who feel like zeroes as they walk by the bell-ringing Santas in front of department stores they feel unworthy to enter.

Talbot especially was gloomy. Christmas presents were impossible, since he had used his savings for the trip to Birmingham after the bombing of the 16th Street Church. His mother and father—chief singer and minister at a Harlem church—made a big deal out of Christmas. There was already the tradition of Talbot showing up on Christmas Eve with a stack of gifts for parents, sisters, cousins, uncles and aunts. He also wanted to get some books for Johnny Ray Slage, the klan kid he had met in Alabama, and to whom he had been sending weekly educational packets.

Cynthia wasn't worried about not having presents when she showed up in her annual holiday trek home. Her problem was the bus ticket. For some reason her mother thought that hitchhiking was the sigil of total depravity. Cynthia was determined to avoid the strained, horrified "Ha! I predicted it!" expression on the mommie brow when she unlocked the kitchen door, having thumbed through winter storms, her room kept perfect with the dolls and teddies of her childhood, door closed against dust, blinds drawn, waiting like a museum exhibit.

Cynthia's usual procedure for cash-scrounge was to band together with friends from the Catholic Worker and sell its newspaper at night on crowded streets. The cover price was a penny, but people would often give a dime or a quarter, and they would divide the extra money between themselves and the Worker. Thus she could come home with up to seven or eight dollars, enough for a week's diet of grains and pasta. She hadn't been able to do anything since the assassination except suffer and pray; in fact, she had come out of her depression only a couple of days ago, and had gone against a longstanding vow never to become a waitress to avoid the humility of home-hitch.

Kliver chided them over their "yule mewl." It was just an ignorant game, he said. "Why do you want to show up falsely prosperous and hand out stupidities wrapped in overpriced paper for hostile relatives who, whatever you brought them, would accept them with the barely inaudible snickers of squares!"

Cynthia and Talbot sat down on Kliver's mattress and smoked a reefer to the background track of jazz from the smashed guts of a radio in a shoebox, while Kliver entertained them with a stream of quick wild tales culled from the life he lived at the intersections of anarcho-pacifist Catholic poetry and the world of small time heroin users.

There was a succession of coded knocks as they talked, mostly tray bag and nickel bag customers. Among them was an N.Y.U. student from the suburbs named Sandy, who arrived in a blue boater's coat with gold buttons and penny loafers polished in oxblood to an antique gloss. His blond hair, already thinning at 20, was cut crewcut short, yet he'd managed to part it and plaster it against his noggin in what was known as the Princeton style.

His cheeks spoke of pink health and his notebooks from chemistry and physics lay beside him on the mattress. It was obvious Sandy hadn't done that much smack. He bought $250 of nickel bags, presents he said for his pals on the

Island. Kliver was very happy, and as soon as Sandy left he peeled off five tens and handed them to Talbot.

Talbot the Great at first refused them, but Kliver insisted. "Get some presents. Wrap them well. Be an American!"

Meanwhile, back in his pad Sam had decided it was premature to worry about poverty till his oat level dropped to around 20 or 25 pounds. Instead he was working on an editorial for the next issue of *The Shriek*. He was dealing with his enemies. "And remember," he typed, "the Egyptian word for asshole is ⸌𓃀𓊖𓏺𓏺𓈖—pekhweyet!—and beginning with this issue each *Shriek of Revolution* shall bestow Golden ⸌𓃀𓊖𓏺𓏺𓈖 Awards." Sam typed a list of bestowees, among them J. Edgar Hoover of the F.B.I., new president Lyndon Johnson, Governor Wallace of Alabama, Bull Connor of the Birmingham police and Morty Kemp, the latter being a theater operator on 2nd Avenue who had attacked Sam in the crowded lobby after a poetry benefit the other night.

He hated making enemies! Yet Sam always found them rising against him. Morty Kemp detested the mix of pacifism, reefer, eleutherarchy, nonviolent direct action and democratic communism promulgated by Thomas in *The Shriek*. It was one of those cases where the offended party overreacts, foaming at the bicuspid—"You try to mollify the masses with sex, drugs and pseudo politics! You know you don't give a damn about the poor! And you're insensitive to the class struggle!"

Sam said nothing at the time, but he was bothered by the charges. One of his secret obsessions in his early years on the East Side was to make lists of friends and enemies. Not that Morty Kemp was such a perfect revolutionary worker, and Sam should lose sleep over his deprecation. The sneers of peers were part of Sam's introduction to the sweet-sour spoon of renown—signing his first autographs, gluing his first book reviews in a scrapbook, kvelling over ads for screenings of his films, learning about the strange sub-world of book and relic collectors, people rushing up gushing with praise in the street to get the latest issue of *The Shriek*, which he always gave away free, and women offering Im-Grat, Uncle Thrills' acronym for immediate gratification.

Sam typed the list of recipients onto the stencil. Then he untied a canvas roll with fobs containing his styluses and engraving tools and began etching the ⸌𓃀𓊖𓏺𓏺𓈖 -hieroglyphics next to each name on the blue film. It gave him such pleasure to calligraph the glyph, say, for "pekh," ⸌𓃀 , the hindquarters of a lion. He was beginning to worry, however, about the spelling for asshole. Was it correct? He didn't want his Egyptian professor, to whom he always sent *The Shriek,* grinning over a goof, so he turned to the stacks of milk crates against the wall containing his Egyptology books, and pulled out a dictionary of Middle Egyptian.

His joy in his Egyptian collection was unbounded! He patted the books, feeling the electric thrill on his fingertips bumping from binder to binder! How he loved the lore of the Nile—the sky above the narrow flood plains along its banks swarming with a vast assortment of deities, and the underground cities of its dead packed with wondrous ceremonies! And the art of the hieroglyph, was there anything more beautiful?

After he'd checked the spelling, Sam tarried at the crates, skimming through old crumbly-edged issues of the Journal of Egyptian Archaeology. He hefted the huge Alan Gardiner *Egyptian Grammar*, and the marvelous books of Wallis Budge, such as *The Papyrus of Ani* and the two-volume Medici Edition of *Osiris and the Egyptian Resurrection*. All of them had a mustiness and dustiness and chippédness that hinted, in themselves, of ancient amulets on natron-packed bones and dusty chambers under the lid of the earth.

He sat in the lotus position on his bamboo mat, the faint December sun beaming upon him past a crisscrossing of clotheslines and wet sheets in the courtyard. He was feeling a paradise *pro tempore.* "This is surely the Three V's!" he shouted, as he pulled forth more books from the crates. By the Three V's he meant Voluntas, Voluptas and Vastitudo—will, thrill and vastness. It gave him a pacing peace, the sort of energized pax that he guessed monks must feel who pace while meditating. At random he opened a facsimile edition of the Ebers Papyrus, a long medical treatise on Egyptian medicine that includes some 811 prescriptions and formulae for treatment of disorders.

By accident Sam's eyes came upon the section on cosmetics—cures for baldness, formulae for wrinkles and outbreaks on the face. Sam read intently—it was intriguing what the Egyptians used! One remedy for wrinkles consisted of "incense cake," whatever that was, wax, olive oil, something called cyperus and fresh milk. Another had bulls-bile in it. Yet another featured "whipped ostrich egg," and runoff of dongwash, that is, water used to wash the genitals.

Sam was particularly fascinated by a wrinkle cream consisting of sea-salt, honey, oil, meal-of-alabaster and crocodile shit. It must be noted that dung of every origin was utilized in Egyptian pharmacology. They even had a medicinal use for fly spots.

He stared at the formula for several minutes. Finally his mouth formed two words in silence—"Christmas rush." Sam saw upon the screen of his visual cortex a jar emblazoned like a photo slide. A jar of Egyptian face cream. It was resting on a shelf in a Greenwich Village store. "Yazzah!" Sam Thomas shouted, jumping to his feet, still carrying the Ebers Papyrus, dancing around his pad, hopping first on one foot, then the other, trying to click his heels together. "I've solved my money problems! Thank you, O Sebek!" Sebek was the Egyptian crocodile deity.

Sam waited impatiently till his heart rate lowered enough that he could sit back down and start sketching ideas for label text, the shapes of jars and so forth on smooth hard sheets of the paper they call Bristol board. He executed a fine likeness of a crocodile beneath which he lettered his product's temporary title,

"The Muffins of Sebek Ancient Egyptian Face Cream & Miracle Toner."

"What do you do with the crocodile dooky?" Sam asked suddenly. He'd gone to the Bronx Zoo and was standing next to the pool where an attendant was cleaning away the crocodilian detritus. Sam looked longingly at the poolside depositions. "I need about 25 pounds. How much?"

At that, the attendant turned to Sam, wondering what sort of vagabond from bonkersville had shown up at the acrid edge of his enclosure. The young man he encountered was wearing a pith helmet and knee-high snake boots. Sam had planned to pose as an expert on African fauna with a legitimate scholarly need for croc-offal, but had quailed.

Sam had watched the keeper for some time before addressing him. There was something balletically hip about the way he was cleaning the enclosure, so Sam gambled. "You see, I'm an inventor. I need it. I'll give you a nickel bag of Panamanian red. I can come back whenever you want."

The attendant kept cleaning the enclosure, acting as if he hadn't heard. Then he turned to Sam. "It's a deal. Better come back in two or three days. I'll gather them into some cans. They'll have a chance to dry."

The next step was walking all over the Lower East Side on jar patrol. He needed at least a hundred, and they had to be cheap—preferably free. He browsed in the junk shops on Houston near the Bowery; he smirched his sleeve cuffs on the edges of supermarket waste bins and dove armpit deep into those huge rectangular debris boxes at construction sites.

There were several containers that came close to what he wanted, among them Skippy peanut butter jars, abandoned for their inelegance, and the jars that had once contained the milky rolls of Vita brand herring, which were too small. Also abandoned were blue glass Noxzema jars. He needed something with a wide mouth so that a hand could easily scoop forth the facesaving Sebek-ian ooze and which was large enough so that he could charge bountifully for it. As primitive as his business sense was, Sam knew that on this project the object was to deal a few at macro rather than many at micro.

He found what he wanted while walking past a car wash on Houston Street, eyes darting like an experienced can diver to any and all garbage locations. There they were! Hundreds of wide-mouth metal-lidded jars that had once contained auto wax—perfect for an ancient Egyptian cosmetic! All he had to do was scrape off the labels and add his own. Sam returned with gunny sacks and loaded up as many as he could carry and trotted back to 11th Street.

The plan called for Sam to pick up the muffins early in the morning before the zoo was open. Sam arrived with newspapers, cord, tape, surgical gloves, oodles of shopping bags and some paralytic grass on credit from Nelson Saite.

Before the keeper's astonished gaze, Sam tamped the chunks into shot-put sized accretions and wrapped each one in newspapers, sprinkling a few drops of attar of roses upon them before sealing the edges with tape. He began filling the shopping bags with the packets till he had twelve, which he tied together into two six-bag bundles, one for each hand. Thus he could walk out of the zoo quite comfortably, if slowly, enjoying the stroll along Fordham Road past Fordham University toward the subway at the Grand Concourse.

It was the rush hour when Sam Thomas shoved himself aboard the D train. The car was packed, yet you'd be surprised how much space can be found when someone presses forward with 12 bags of lizard shit. The train took him to 14th Street where he switched to the crosstown subway to 1st Avenue, then walked up the steps toward home.

Sam didn't look behind him, as he usually did, before entering his building. As soon as the door began to swing inward, someone shoved his shoulder from behind so that he lurch-stumbled upon the ▧-patterned tile floor common to hallways all over the East Side. He turned around, expecting to be robbed, and recognized a famous team of narks known as Mutt and Jeff that specialized in busting beatniks.

One was short and chubby, with a high blood pressure face and his pants cuffs rolled almost to his sock tops. The other was tall with the pits of pox on sunken cheeks and a knife scar cutting upward from his left eyelid through his eyebrow. Mutt and Jeff kept their collar count high by interdicting beatnik pot traffic, but they were extremely weak on heroin. Not long afterwards they would be busted for peddling dope from the evidence lockers. For now, however, they were knotting their ties high upon the arm of power, breathing hard and cackling with pleasure at cornering the overburdened Sam Thomas.

"OK, Thomas, let's have a talk in the hallway."

Sam looked carefully at them. He hated being alone in hallways with plain-clothes cops. He'd heard stories. One of them had his hand on his hip near his holster, so Sam went into a yes-sir grovel, thinking they might shoot him. It was like being mugged as they shoved and jostled him to the wall, patting his legs and pockets for weapons.

He was preparing to collapse to the floor, as he would have at a peace demonstration, when the shorter one with the muffin'd cuffs said, "We saw you leaving Saite's pad a couple of hours ago. What's in the bags? You delivering?"

Sam abandoned the floor-collapse. Instead he fought back the urge to smile, and replied, "It's some stuff for face cream."

"Sure it is," Mutt answered. "Open them up, Thomas. You'd better not ever lie to us. We know where you live."

Sam untied one of the six-shopping-bag bundles and tore away the coverings to expose the muffins. The unmistakable waft of perfumed crocodile dooky crowded the hallway.

Jeff became excited. "Look at those bricks of hash, huh Thomas? Looks like you and Saite were going to start a little business."

Mutt stepped back about five feet and pulled his revolver. "Check it out, Jeff."

Jeff picked one up. "This smells like perfume or spice. Maybe they added stuff to cut it."

Sam was beginning to relax. He said, "I guess you should do something to make sure, huh, officer?"

"Don't get wise with me, beatnik creep!" Jeff snorted. He brought the chunk to his lips and took a small nibble. Words cannot adequately depict the ensuing facial grimace as he spat it out and hurled the rest to the floor. "What is this shit!?"

It became one of those legendary moments—the day Sam Thomas got the muffin of Sebek into the nark's mouth. Sam could no longer keep from laughing. He pinched himself to keep from guffawing to the floor. He didn't want them beating him up. He spoke in a half cough, half laugh. "You heard—harf! harf!—of the Egyptian god Sebek? Well,—harf! harf!—it's a gift from Sebek— harf! harf! harf!"

That confused them. It reminded the officers that after all they were dealing with an imbalanced space cadet. Without speaking they left Sam Thomas in the hallway and Sam walked elated up the steps to prepare for the Christmas rush.

Sam had already soaked the labels from the autowax jars and had put them on the fire escape to dry. He'd cadged a piece of alabaster from a sculpture supply house and began hammering it into meal-of-alabaster, an ingredient of the cream, on his porcelainized bathtub cover. The Ebers Papyrus was silent on relative proportions so he had to experiment, using one of his Yum bowls, which, as the crocodile skuz began to work into the cracks, he decided to retire from food service. He realized that it had to resemble actual American facial products or no one would buy it.

He lit a row of candles along the kitchen drainboard and taped a flashlight on the underside of the cabinet above the tub so that it beamed down upon the tub cover and the wooden bowl. He added some meal-of-alabaster, oil, some honey, the sea-salt, a chunk of muff', plus, for fragrance, oils of hyacinth and columbine. To his distress the mixture lacked body. Oats were the answer. A toss of raw oats fluffed it up nicely and gave it consistency. By increasing the oats he found he could decrease the crocodility. He mashed and whipped the improvements into a proper puffy elation. Its color, however, was a most unappealing tanny gray, so he added blue food coloring. And there it was.

The sink was too small for the entire batch so he lifted away the covering and sacrificed his tub. He unwrapped the remaining depositions of Sebek and dropped them within. He added the alabaster frags, the oil, a gallon of honey, the hyacinth and columbine, the dye, and most of his remaining oatmeal. The ingredients did not automatically fall into commixture. He had to exert considerable downward vectoring in order to mash it all into the proper glopitude. This was accomplished by using his galoshes. He rested on his knees at tub's edge and thrust his arms down into the galoshes, using his hands as feet, and then performed a sort of plodding dance, working it slowly into a shiny blue mass. His speed increased, passing "Twist, baby, twist" on the way to "Tutti Frutti," when Sam heard a knock at the door and left the galoshes in place, withdrawing his arms, and lumbered over to answer. It was a very upset Talbot the Great, carrying a stack of yule-trimmed presents which he tossed clunkingly upon Sam's bamboo floor mat.

Sam clicked on the flashlight above the tub and urged Talbot, "Look at my ancient Egyptian face cream!"

Talbot stood dejectedly in the gloom-flicker of the row of candles and was too distracted to give anything but a quick glance at the boots in the blue. "Sandy's dead," he said.

"Who's Sandy?"

"A cat I met—an N.Y.U. student—who bought a few c's worth of skag the other day from Kliver. I happened to be there at the time of the deal. I was broke and Kliver just walked over and gave me fifty dollars from Sandy's money. I used it all on Christmas presents.

"I'm going through horrible changes over it, man, because I just visited Kliver and he said the cat died yesterday of an o.d. out in Great Neck."

Sam tried to change the subject. "What'd you get for Johnny Ray Slage?"

Talbot pointed at some packages. "The Bob Dylan album, a subscription to Liberation Magazine and Martin King's *Letter from the Birmingham Jail*."

Sam was excited. "Terrific presents to help shape a klan boy's mind!"

"But I can't give them to him," Talbot said.

"Why not?"

"Because I just bought a bunch of Christmas presents with Sandy's death. It would be disgraceful to give them out."

"What are you going to do with them?"

"Two things. Either I'm going to throw them in the East River or into the garbage pail. I also thought of leaving them anonymously in the hall for the kids in the building. In any case, I can't have them in my pad. They're driving me crazy."

All Sam could think of saying was, "The lily grows from the burro's bones," hardly a sentence of consolation. Talbot split, telling Sam at the door, "We're going to have to force Kliver to give up junk. Tie him down to his bed. Get him into a hospital. Something."

Sam agreed. "Right! We'll lock him into a human Kick Grid! We'll draw up a list and guard him around the clock till he turkeys out of it!"

Sam jotted a reminder in his notebook to deliver the presents to Talbot's parents in Harlem, and to send the klan kid's presents to Alabama. Then he went back to the cream.

He was almost finished packing and sealing the jars when Cynthia Pruitt arrived after her shift at the House of Nothingness. One minute she was grumpy, the next depressed, and she was singularly underenthused when Sam shined the light upon the wavy surface of blue pharmaceutical in the tub.

She hated the job! Each hour of toil had lowered her natural idealism. It was spoiling the surge of religion she'd felt in the days after JFK's assassination. She'd always loved the House of Nothingness, loved to read poetry there, loved to treat it as an all night scrounge-lounge for fun and play. It was humiliating to have to wait on the same people with whom she had sported at table, her knuckles wet with spilled coffee and table grit, watching them in their roles as careless louts.

And the grunge of it! "Did you ever try to clean up a plate of brown rice and seaweed someone has dropped into a sea of white sand?" she asked. One of her duties was wiping and mopping the men's room. The hair, the dirt, the incontinence! It wasn't just the derelicts that stumbled in from Tompkins Park! Your ordinary run-of-the-reefer beatnik would spray the rim and floor with urine as if he were having a seizure at the same time! Cynthia was disgusted.

And the tip-clips! You couldn't leave a tip amidst the clutter on the oak for more than ten seconds. She had caught a poet with seven mimeographed books in print walking sneakily among empty tables making mongoose-quick tip-goniff scooping gestures. "I'm going to quit this fucking job the minute I raise my half of the rent and the ticket to Vermont," she said.

Sam believed one of the few things lighting the path from the downer trough was eros, so he helped Cynthia off with her coat, and led her to the divan. He opened her blouse to rub some of the cream into the cavity between the tops of her breasts. "Try it," he said. "It's the oldest beauty formula in civilization. Not that you need a whit of improvement. For you, St. Cynthia, are be-uuuuu-ti-fulll." That was one of the love names Sam had given during her month of prayer.

Cynthia lowered her chin to star at the shiny blue grease. "What's in it?"

Sam recited the ingredients.

She tried to stay calm. "You mean I've got crocodile shit on my tits?"

Sam nodded.

Her anger was sudden, like a lit glaze of gas on a flat rock. She ripped the flashlight from where it was taped above the tub and stood with it at the sink, running water, rubbing the saurian sludge from her chest till it blushed an abraded red.

Cynthia's reaction was a surprise to Sam. It had not occurred to him that anyone would hesitate to apply the pomade from an Egyptian papyrus to their body. For a few moments Sam pondered the ethicality of the project. Was it fully in tune with the concept of Gandhian nonviolence to foist upon the public a product, a component of which had come from the rear of a lizard?

The moment of doubt was brief. Sam felt a surge of *faith* in the Ebers Papyrus. These formulae represented compilations of folk remedies tested through the centuries. He thought of the well-known women of Egypt who might have used the Muffins of Sebek Ancient Egyptian Face Cream & Miracle Toner. Hatshepsut! Nefertiti! Queen Tiy!

Cynthia stood in a silent rage, refusing to face him. Sam walked to the tub and scooped up mighty handfuls and pressed them to his face so that he looked like a deflated blue soccer ball. "Here!" he shouted. "This is an efficacious ancient formula! The Egyptians built up their medical knowledge slowly and carefully over the course of thousands of years! This is good stuff!"

Then he did what he did so well. He fell to his knees on the bamboo mat and apologized with molten words. They went to Stanley's where they spent some of her bus ticket money for calming vodka, then Sam walked her home to Ludlow Street and hurried back to finish the face cream.

Her hostile reaction to the contents made Sam meditate on the name, the Muffins of Sebek Ancient Egyptian Face Cream & Miracle Toner. Perhaps he should lessen the emphasis on the muffins? The title did seem somewhat ponderous and quackish, like one of those blue glass bottles of Dr. Fromkin's Mandrake Bitters from the 19th century.

It was time to publish the labels. One of the finest stylus-on-stencil artists anywhere, Sam bent down over the stencil, carefully scratching its surface, but not so deeply as to pierce it, using his assortment of very thin round-tipped styluses and icepick sharp engraver's tools.

"What a label!" Sam exclaimed as he executed the final tiny Eye of Horus, his flashlight wedged between his knees and protruding upward to form a small round light table. He smoothed the stencil upon the drum of his Speed-o-Print mimeo, poured ink into the portal, and had labels in ten minutes. He was up till dawn, hand coloring each label, and gluing them neatly onto the jars.

Next he printed cards which explained how the formula rested upon an ancient papyrus, a formula proven effective over 3,000 years ago due to the powerful effect of oils, grains and what Sam delicately described as "essence of Sebek." He punched holes in the cards, threaded them with loops of Christmas ribbon and suspended one from each jar's neck.

It was ready. The rest of the project was push and shove, and shove Sam did, wheedling, beseeching, begging his wares aboard the shelves of Village stores right at the time when trembly-fingered shoppers, determined to spend, were jammed as tightly as lambs around a bale of hay.

Within a week all hundred jars were sold, giving him enough for the rent, to turn his lights on and to buy some paper for the next *Shriek*. Lie quiet, O Sebek.

A Lower East Side Poem

BY MIGUEL PIÑERO

Just once before I die
I want to climb up on a
tenement sky
to dream my lungs out till
I cry
then scatter my ashes thru
the Lower East Side.

So let me sing my song tonight
let me feel out of sight
and let all eyes be dry
when they scatter my ashes thru
the Lower East Side.

From Houston to 14th Street
from Second Avenue to the mighty D
here the hustlers & suckers meet
the faggots and freaks will all get
high
on the ashes that have been scattered
thru the Lower East Side.

There's no other place for me to be
there's no other place that I can see
there's no other town around that
brings you up or keeps you down
no food little heat sweeps by

fancy cars & pimps' bars & juke saloons
& greasy spoons make my spirits fly
with my ashes scattered thru the
Lower East Side ...

A thief, a junkie I've been
committed every known sin
Jews and Gentiles ... Bums and Men
of style ... run away child
police shooting wild ...
mother's futile wail ... pushers
making sales ... dope wheelers
& cocaine dealers ... smoking pot
streets are hot & feed off those who bleed to
death ...

all that's true
all that's true
all that is true
but this ain't no lie
when I ask that my ashes be scattered thru
the Lower East Side.

So here I am, look at me
I stand proud as you can see
pleased to be from the Lower East
a street fighting man
a problem of this land
I am the Philosopher of the Criminal Mind
a dweller of prison time
a cancer of Rockefeller's ghettocide
this concrete tomb is my home
to belong to survive you gotta be strong
you can't be shy less without request
someone will scatter your ashes thru
the Lower East Side.

I don't wanna be buried in Puerto Rico
I don't wanna rest in long island cemetery
I wanna be near the stabbing shooting
gambling fighting & unnatural dying
& new birth crying
so please when I die...
don't take me far away
keep me near by
take my ashes and scatter them thru out
the Lower East Side...

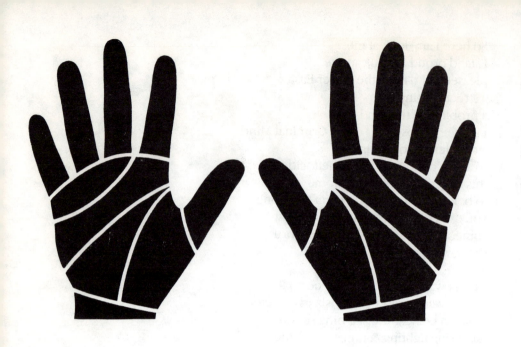

Watch the Closing Doors

BY OLIVIA BEENS

THE NUMBER TWO—IT WAS 10 P.M. ON A WEEKDAY night. I was tired. The train was brightly lit and crowded. I looked over and saw him. A brown paper bag at his feet, a bottle of wine perhaps. I think he unscrewed the cap and took a swig. I asked him to move over. He looked at me and thoughtfully considered the situation. He didn't care to be disturbed but I suppose he found me to be agreeable enough. I was lost in thought, something comparable to space flight, I think. The light was strange and the motion severe. I felt his leg. He was making physical contact with me. I felt every inch of his thigh against mine. He smelt of wine, labor and dirty clothes. His touch was familiar, like a lover who snuggles against you in the night for more. I didn't mind. It was friendly, intriguing and sexual. He asked me something. We began to talk and laugh a bit. The other passengers started to take notice of us. He wanted to spend more time with me but I was getting off at the next stop. I felt wonderful. I didn't mind the usual maze-like atmosphere of the station. A woman approached me and said, "Pardon me, dear, for being so inquisitive, but are you a social worker?" I laughed and told her I was an artist.

Have you not met Michelangelo Leonardo! Or was it Raphael?

DOUBLE A

It was one of those perfect December days; bright and crisp. There was snow on the ground and the sunlight made everything shimmer. Steve and I were going to the Museum of Natural History. He wanted to see the Venus of Willendorf and I wanted to buy a book about sea-monsters for my young son. It was two days before Christmas. The subway car was crowded with shoppers but it was not oppressive as in usual rush hour traffic. I spotted a young Hispanic woman with a bottle of Budweiser at her feet. Steve and I conversed as we looked at the passengers. Out of the corner of my eye I saw her stand up, pull her pants down, squat and piss . . . right there on the floor. As the train swerved the river formed tributaries. The passengers simply lifted their feet, allowing the river to flow freely.

I saw yellow and purple sea-monsters rise from the foam as in a primordial myth.

MANHATTAN

A strange but familiar scent filled the subway car. It was a hot Sunday evening in mid-July. I was traveling with my young son and everything was sticky. The man who sat to the right of us had braces on his legs, carried two metal canes and read the Post. A proper middle-aged woman sat opposite us reading the Times. She wore an interesting necklace which, I think, doubled as a time piece. Sitting diagonally across from us in the two seater between the doors and the entrance to the next compartment was a couple, quite obviously in love. The scent permeated the compartment. It was sweet and pungent, quickly becoming repugnant, like overripe fruit. I looked over past the steel shanks and saw her: she was huge, took up two seats, was muttering to herself. And she was completely naked from the waist down. Immediately, I recognized the scent. The man next to us hobbled away with great difficulty. He was thoroughly repulsed. The woman sitting across from us kept repeating, "I don't believe it! I just don't *believe* it!" The couple giggled to one another. And I tried to contain my tears and my laughter. It was a long journey through the tunnel to Brooklyn. The doors opened and she got up to exit but they closed before she could. She banged on the doors. "ROBERT REDFORD, BURT REYNOLDS, PAUL NEWMAN, OPEN THE DOORS!" But nothing happened. Again she banged, "ROBERT REDFORD, BURT REYNOLDS, PAUL NEWMAN, OPEN THE DOORS!" And the doors opened. She exited and we all breathed a sigh of relief.

She was the Venus of Willendorf in search of her modern day hero.

TAKE THE A TRAIN

She had to have it! She just had to!

She planned it all out. Put on her jungle dress. Punched holes into her red plaid traveling case and headed Uptown on the A train. She walked down 125th Street. Went straight to Blumberg's Department Store. And went downstairs to the Pet Shop. She waited for the school children to leave. Opened the cage. Put her hand inside around his waist. He held onto the bars with his feet and hands, screaming. Now, she knew why he was called a Howler. She yanked harder, freeing him from the bars, and shoved him into the traveling case. Quickly, she headed for the stairs when someone grabbed her arm. She hit him with the case, until she realized that he, the monkey, that is, might get hurt. They brought her upstairs to a small room, questioned her, lectured her and made her sign something. She promised never to return again. The store detective told her that she needed to see a psychiatrist.

"Honey," he said, "What you really want is a BABY."

SHAKIN'

Shakin'...She just couldn't stop shakin'. My eyes latched on to her but she never noticed my stare. She was too busy lookin' for something. I watched her through the mirror of the Chock Full O'Nuts on 34th Street near Herald Square. Her eyes darted around the joint. I wondered how she got that way—hair all greasy, ripped clothes, kind of dirty and always shakin'. There was something familiar about her. She reminded me of someone, an old friend, maybe? She was my age, same coloring and size. Perhaps we went to school together, or maybe I saw her somewhere—the subway?...Grand Central Station?...or the ladies room at Penn Station? Her eyes finally focused on something. It was a cup of coffee, half empty. She maneuvered her body to it, gulped it down, picked a butt out of the ashtray, had trouble lighting it and took a drag. I finished my cup and headed for the F train. I couldn't stop thinking about her and her shakin' sack-like body. I began to tremble and wondered why I was thinking about her so much. I missed my stop. Got up to change trains, saw my reflection in the door and I was shakin'...I wondered how she got that way—hair all greasy, ripped clothes, kind of dirty and shakin'.

She Just Couldn't Stop Shakin'.

Here

BY JOHN FARRIS

THERE IS A LOT OF VIOLENCE IN ALPHABETTOWN. I've got plenty of lumps & bumps to prove it too, loops & curves, high points & depressions, teeth missing, scars above both eyes, a big hole (another curve—or even depression) in my pride, the knowing that, alas, I'm not invincible. That's what I want to be—invincible—but I'm afraid it's an impossible task. Too many people bumping around. I was walking past Vazac's the other night, saw a crowd you wouldn't believe, some swell, drawn there probably by the promise of fine food, fat roasts & rumps; I decided what the hell, pop in, you can't lose anything even if it is the fucking Mets—the problem with whom being it's just a little difficult to get the attention I need for my own interviews if Dwight Gooden has just thrown the greatest curve in the history of baseball, who wants to discuss how brilliant I am—as there must have been a thousand eyes in there, all blue, all riveted in one direction. My own eyes are brown & hardly what they used to be though I hate to wear my glasses unless I'm driving; couldn't see anything except two black guys, shirtless & in shorts, pounding the holy cowwalking shit out of each other or at least one of them was pounding the shit out of the other while that one appeared in need of a good antihistamine his eyes were so puffy & red, similar to the way my own were winter before last when I was kicking the shit out of Patrick's ass because of a looping curve Freida'd thrown at me with all her flaky shit & missing with a looping curve of my own had hit that ice, my body curling downward through the air, arcing outward as I tried to save myself what ignominy, the ignominy of horns, bells, flutes, birdies—tweet tweet—that mysterious dark room all the great heavyweights talk about (a good boxer is a psychologist too) having come back from, the most horrible impression in my forehead of that family that won't go away ever even though they are nice people, this mise-en-scene; skyhooks, flattering Arabs, impoverished Jamaicans, Bajans, Nicaraguans, Dominicans, Mexicans, Trinidadians, Guatemaltecos, Salvadoreños, Puertorriqueños, Haitians, Martiniquans, Panamanians, Brazilians & just plain old dog-type American niggers up there dukin' it out with no clothes on except some shorts & sneakers, silk too, with names like Everlast written over the solar plexus; nexus: that skyhook, it was something—the very opposite of a bolo—nothing classic about it except maybe it came from some god, somebody you didn't take care of because you didn't even know they were up there, some gimp, somebody with a big wart with gigantic hairs coming out of it, the last supplicant after an illustrious career & you're just dog-tired, need sleep, you're in no condition to be fuckin' around with this guy's got such superb muscle tone he seems kinetic, positively strobic in how now you see him, now you don't, to see where what he hit you with came from as you weren't serious enough about whatever it was you said for it to have come to this were you dealing on a rational level, bozo, he smacked your tobacco-rotten teeth out, made both your lips gigantic & red, put a desperate grin on your chalk-white face, gave you peepers for real plus stamped walking papers, big headlines: some clown at Vazac's Polish Hall got his ass kicked for fucking with Reymundo del Mundo, put a clown hat on his ass, gave him a beard & big red ears, put him on a little donkey in case he got tired of walking before I recognized the combatants to be the former heavyweight champion of the world & my little friend Michael who said, Hey, come on—he never wanted to hurt anybody ever—it was his brother put him up to this, he couldn't have gotten out of it for less than eight to ten million dollars finish da palooka or not, this was Vazac Hall, we'd pay with our blood to see something like that, anything; that's why we came here in the first place, made a beeline here; beerline, that is.

So it's over. So I'm walking across town (like I was walking across town the night four Italians jumped me, smart ass told me I'd dropped my nose for no reason at all & I told him it was his mother's nose I'd dropped crotch-high, to which he, being a Wop (I've heard that means without papers) naturally replied he'd fuck me up & when I threw him into the gate surrounding St. Stanislaus School heard his boys coming up on me, plucked him & hung him up before me like a demon shield for my life; for their sport. Some trade. John Farris for four nameless guys without papers & nothing to do on the weekend, a baga-

telle, a French friend called it & a Polish guy in Tompkins Square Park told me
he'd been out of Poland only two weeks & there was only classical music,
meaning more violence; such opinion. I told him, Bullshit, muhfuggah, you just
got out of Poland where they don't let you listen to shit but a mazurka Chopin
claimed & put both the lights out & the radio off at curfew, so what do you
know, bitch, bitch, bitch, we got good music around here to which replied,
Puerto Rican music? & I said, hell no, I'm not talkin' about no fuckin' Puerto
Rican music having just heard Billy Bang being very violent with some funk,
kickin' it dead in the ass with that little violin of his just because it tried to be all
harmelodic, that's all, wants people to jerk around like they got a boot or two up
their stiff ass whether they think they like this stuff or not when I felt a blow
behind my ear would've felled an ox were I not so familiar with the nature of
this particular beastie & a little Borinqueño darted out from behind me said,
Jive muhfuggah, is your black ass talkin' about Puerto Ricans & I lunged at his
diminutive ass like a two-ton locomotive clipped again by an apparition, a shadow, & it's four guys again, something about me and the number four, but they
don't bunch up like those dump wops so I can take advantage of them, no.
These guys spread out amoeba-like, break bottles, stab at me, wait for my guard
to drop, so I get down, I mean really down, hop over these guys like a ninja,
come down about thirty yards away slapping rubber, thinking some good advice: "A good run beats a bad stand any day," ask George Custer, when a friend
appeared, so I booked to a trash bin, found a good piece of bench slat about
four feet long & hopped back but my friend had scared them so it was over by
then, they were reduced to explaining. They said I'd maligned them as Puerto
Ricans. My friend said I shouldn't have done that. I said, shit, this is America, I
can talk about the President, yo' mama, but nobody was listening anymore. I
don't know where that Polish guy went with his shit; he must've really been the
devil.

   There is another kind of violence: My landlord pulled the main support
beam out of the building adjoining mine. He says I've got to get out quick. I
don't know where I'm going to go. I hate Flatbush.

The Day John Left

BY EMILY XYZ

COLD, SILVERY DAY AT THE END OF FALL, 1985. The painted colors of the buildings across the street, across every street, glowed like warm coils in the revolving rays of gold light, and the sheetmetal windows had a hard, leaden, blue sheen. Heroin dealers clamored for business three floors down. Today my friend John has left all this and is in a van full of Velvet Underground records, heading towards Massachusetts.

New York suited him. For years he lived in its blackness and grime, wore its greyed-down colors and its dark glasses, watched its eerie scurrying, walked among its painted painted painted woods and holed walls and old-fashioned machinery, picked musical instruments from the garbage and pictures from the street vendors. Abused its drugs, amused it, wasted its time.

Now it has come the time to do something else; and so he takes everything he has, he is, he has been, and seals it into boxes and metal crates, piles it in a van and drives it all away to a big house in New England.

A fine old Lower East Side tradition is to have a rock 'n' roll band. My own band is gone, being now again what it was in the beginning of time, me and a guy on guitar. After three years we emerged from the mess of wrong drummers and bass players and tiny illegal clubs and desolate rehearsal, to stand more or less at the same place we started, and stare at the big 0 we made getting here.

My recurring fantasy, absurd, possible, is that I will one day come home to find a woman in a mink coat standing in the living-room ordering workmen about, gallery guide in one hand and an interminable lease in the other. This won't happen to John in his big house in Massachusetts. Remember what winter in a house was like: Space. Big rooms (not factory, not warehouse) full of chilly air. Days a glistening tapestry worked in deep cold and deep snow and deep, brilliant blue, blue of every shade, changing every hour; glazed rivers and wide wind, white with snow.

I wrote this to remember you, John, as you were in New York and as New York was, on the 14th day of December 1985, with thin snow flitting across the sheetmetal windows; with a low plane droning through the sky and traffic somehow quiet; with your empty apartment lying still and wondering, apprehensive over the woman in mink; and with the light growing shinier and sharper as it fails, falling like a long knife-blade down the block; and knowing that my time for starting over is here, and here, and that to sing at all means to stay here and sing old things all over again. Sweet Jane plays. You travel, your guitars piled in back. Over us both the sky is revolving, as though giant birds were passing overhead, over and over, crossing the land and heading out to sea.

SEX AND SURVIVAL

1. She was young and she had come, she realized, to think of sex as a survival skill. Not as a video-game-type battle of wits, as she had at seventeen, when she started; not as a stalking-of-prey into the wilds of Escape, as adults do; but as the last checkpoint on the road to being left alone by people in whom her interest had waned, or against whom fear and anger had risen in her. This young woman used to consider herself a little promiscuous, now she was the opposite: because promiscuity wanted sex and *had* sex, and she merely waved sex through, as a border guard would a clean car. She maintained her peace of mind. Her name was Mary.

Early one morning in the fall a couple years ago, Mary had been awakened by a noise near her bed. She opened her eyes and went to sit up, but a man pushed her back down and set the point of his knife into her neck. The knife was the brightest thing in the room. He said he was looking for money but felt her up anyway while tying her wrists together and stuffing a dirty sock in her mouth. There was no money there. Mary knew she would be raped when he finished looking around and found nothing. If she was lucky, he wouldn't cut her. That would be bad, if he cut her. She wanted him to rape her and leave. He didn't seem irrational. He seemed to think he was having sex. Took the sock out of her mouth, kissed her, took his time. Outside the sky was going from sapphire-blue to pearl white.

No one understood why she didn't make a big deal out of it. Friends warned Mary that unless she let her feelings out, they would disappear into the depths of her mind only to surface years later in some disastrous form, like a psychological Creature from the Black Lagoon. Mary said she didn't have time for a breakdown right now and since she honestly felt OK, would prefer to just get past the whole episode. Friends thought she was being incredibly brave, but Mary knew all she'd done was something she'd often done before in answer to her self-posed riddle. Why should I sleep with you, that is. To get to the other side.

2. Mary sat at a table in a gorgeous restaurant with three adults. One was the married man with whom she was supposed to be having an affair. The early summer air was warm and lush. The food was rich. The conversation was like a dust cloud from a building being sandblasted. Reaganomics. Ex-husbands and wives. Mary lifted her water glass. Her friend had given her a jade ring earlier that night, even though she begged him not to give her presents. To him this was an adventure. Extramarital fun. She knew that all his friends thought she was hip, smart, marvelous. They were as bored as he was.

She pondered ways to walk out. But then they all finished their coffee and stood up, saying what fun it had been and how nice it was to meet you Mary after all we've heard about you. I'll just bet you've heard about me, Mary was thinking. Changed my perspective, woke me up, not like any other woman I ever. That sort of thing. She smiled back, and she and her man left hand in hand and got in a cab. He insisted on seeing her home. He came in. Obviously, this was to be it. They had never yet had sex. All right. It was done in less than an hour. After that, they didn't see each other again. She was grateful for having come out of that restaurant with all her wits intact.

3. They had insisted they were friends, friends, friends; and here they were in bed together. And it was very late; and Mary was genuinely sleepy. A long day was coming in from the east, fast, and she knew it, and this boy would not let up. She understood about being nineteen and all that, but her life depended on sleep and he didn't know what he was doing and might take hours. In the midst of some extravagant, unintelligible passion, Mary whispered something to him and his whispered reply was, I'd love it. In two minutes flat he was frozen solid, gasping for air, coming onto her back teeth; in another two minutes he was out cold. Mary got up quietly in the dark, poured water into her mouth from the faucet, spit into the sink and went back to bed.

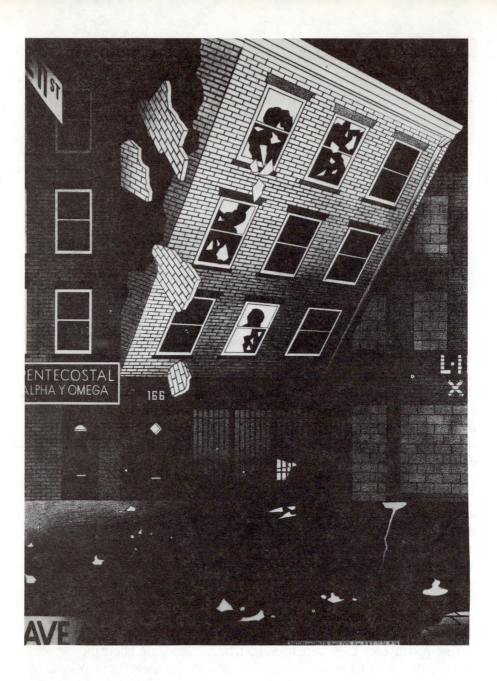

Duke and Jill

BY RON KOLM

UKE AND JILL DO DRUGS. THEY LIVE ON THE corner of Avenue A and 10th Street, in a mostly burnt-out building. Duke is originally from Wisconsin. Jill is from Wisconsin, too. They don't have much else in common.

Bad things keep happening to them. Their best friend, a junky, rents a truck from a company on Lafayette Street, backs it up over the curb, kicks in their apartment door, and takes all their stuff. The TV, the stereo, even their beat-up couch. He knows they'll be out, getting loaded in a neighborhood bar, trying to score some coke. In fact, they're waiting for him to show up with some reasonable blow.

Duke is pissed. He buys a gun, a .38 caliber, used, but still workable, from a guy he knows on the street. Duke and Jill don't fight much the next couple of weeks—she doesn't trust Duke not to shoot her if the going gets too hot. So things chill out for awhile.

One night Duke is sitting around getting loaded. In that condition he hears a banging on the hastily repaired door. He gets his gun and tucks it into his belt, and opens the door, unbolting a newly installed double-bar police lock.

The guy at the door turns out to be a friend, a member of a crypto-punk band he likes a lot.

Wow, you got a gun, the friend says.

Yeah, but it's not loaded, Duke replies. He points the gun at the ceiling, and pulls the trigger. The hammer clicks. I just keep it around to scare Jill—keep her in line, he laughs. Actually, I got it to blow away the scumbag who stole our stuff. If I ever see his ass in the neighborhood he's gone.

Man, let me see that thing, his friend says, excited by the unusual toy. He points the gun at a boarded up window and pulls the trigger. The hammer clicks again. He giggles and aims the gun at his temple, Deer hunter, he says, and pulls the trigger. A bright flash of orange sound bounces around the nearly empty room, stunning Duke and momentarily blinding him.

After the police leave, Jill calls all their friends to tell them the news. She has to shout to be heard above the sound of Duke vacuuming the dried blood off their shag carpet.

DUKE AND JILL HAVE A PARTY

The rent was going up. Someone had died in their apartment. It seemed like a good time to split. So Duke and Jill packed their stuff and moved east. To Avenue D.

They decided to have a party to celebrate their new place. Duke bought a couple of six-packs and some bags of chips, and Jill made dip. Duke also borrowed some tapes from a buddy. Mostly Latin-type dance music. That was about it.

They put out the word, and maybe twenty people showed up. Brought some bottles, and a generous amount of reefer. There wasn't much conversation because, really, there wasn't much to talk about. Everyone just sat around getting loaded.

Jill's old boyfriend, Arnie, was there. He kept his eye on her and, when Duke disappeared into the next room with a young thing, they got together. The party got wild. Everyone took their clothes off. Jill took pictures.

Everyone agreed that they were having a really good time. So it was a real bummer when, later, the developed rolls of film got mailed to Jill's mother by mistake.

THE MURGATROYDS LEAVE TOWN

Duke was back on the street again, dealing to pay the rent. He had a pretty good connection—no money up front. But Duke would push his nickels and dimes, and then blow his profits on coke. He couldn't seem to get ahead. And the neighborhood was getting hot. The cops were having a field day out there. He knew all sorts of people on the block who'd been busted.

Jill, as usual, came up with the solution. Why not make one really big buy, she said, a *really* big buy, and I don't mean reefer either, and then chill out for awhile. Maybe take a trip.

So Duke hit his connection for twenty thousand dollars worth of cocaine. I've got to get out of this grind, he told the man. The man nodded sympathetically and put his arm around Duke's shoulder. Good luck, he said tenderly, you know you're like a son to me. Just don't fuck this one up. He squeezed Duke's arm. A little too hard.

Duke took the stuff home and dumped it on the kitchen table. Jill seemed to have a little trouble comprehending the size and shape of it at first. Then she started jumping up and down. Let's celebrate, she said. Okay, Duke said, but we can only do a little.

Jill (the name Murgatroyd hardly seemed to suit her) finished a second, then a third line. Honey, are you sure nobody followed you home, she asked Duke. I don't think so, he replied, polishing off his fifth. Though there was a strange dude hanging out on the corner, he said, frowning.

Jill crawled over to the window and peeked out. I see him, Duke, he's down there. The cops must have set you up. We'll be thrown in jail. I don't want to go to jail for the rest of my life, she wailed.

One thing led to another, and before either of them realized what they were doing the cocaine had been flushed down the toilet. Jill crawled back to the window. The man on the corner had left.

Knowing that they'd never be able to pay back the man, and that a low-level contract would be taken out on Duke (broken knees, fingers, etc.), they decided to flee.

We'll have to change our names, said Duke, maybe to Smith or something like that.

Thank God, thought Jill.

DUKE MAKES THE ART SCENE

Duke was beginning to feel out of it walking around in his own neighborhood. It seemed as if most of the people he passed on the street had more money than he did—everyone was wearing expensive costumes and doing strange things with their hair. The junkies he'd known from years ago were all drifting away—and there was a new Gap clothing store on the corner of 9th Street and 2nd Avenue.

Duke figured he'd better come up with some sort of career while there was still time. He didn't want to end up like the sun-baked winos who slept on the sidewalk. So he put his mind to work.

One night, while cadging a bunch of free drinks at an art gallery opening, it came to him. A plastic-coated sheet listing the prices of the paintings was lying on a table and Duke noticed the amounts with astonishment. Holy shit, he said out loud, I could do better stuff than this.

He read up on the subject in a special issue of the *East Village Eye* which he 'borrowed' from the Gem Spa. Duke also 'borrowed' a candy bar at the same time.

It seemed that a well-known graffiti artist was tucking away quite a bundle, so Duke decided to head in that direction. He 'borrowed' a can of white spray paint from a hardware store and let himself through an exit gate at the 8th Street subway stop. Pay your fare, the token booth clerk yelled at him.

Duke walked along the platform til he found an unused ad space covered with black paper. He started to draw some stick figures doing exotic things to each other only to be rudely interrupted by a big hand on his shoulder. Get outa here before I shove that can up your can, a T.A. cop snarled at him. Having read about what the cops did to another graffiti artist in that same issue of the *Eye*, Duke didn't stick around to argue the point. He split at great speed, his hopes of making an instant fortune in the art world evaporating.

The next day, on the way to his usual selling spot outside the Cooper Union Building, he came across a broken generator armature in a dumpster. It looked like an interesting piece of junk, so he took it along.

He carefully arranged his stuff on the blanket, displaying each item to its best advantage, and then sat back to examine his new find. The afternoon dragged by. A couple of rowdy NYU kids looked at the girlie mags. Duke was bored. He sat in the sun idly fooling around with the armature. He attached it to a splintered piece of pegboard and signed his name on it with the white spray paint. He tossed the result aside and sat back on his blanket, tired and disgusted with the world.

About five minutes later a limo driving by stopped abruptly and a trendy looking fellow leaped out and rushed over toward Duke's spot. I must have that piece for my collection, he cried. He scooped up the mounted armature and asked Duke how much it cost.

Five hundred bucks, Duke replied coolly, not batting an eye.

JILL GETS FASHIONABLE

Jill was tired of being called a hippie by the punks on St. Mark's Place. Her shag had long since grown out and lost its shape, and her jeans had patches on the patches. She felt totally out of it. And worse, she was beginning to feel old.

Damn, she thought, I'd better take some steps fast, or Duke's gonna start looking around.

She wandered into a neighborhood bar to think things over and have a drink or two. She only intended to have a couple of beers. Jill was trying to save money. She'd been laid-off from her job at the Novelty Company. And she only had seventy-five dollars left of her severance pay.

Many drinks later, she made up her mind. She'd do a complete overhaul! And with her courage fortified by a large dose of alcohol she stumbled across 7th Street toward the Astor Place Haircutters.

What'll it be, Miss, the barber asked her.

I don't know, she slurred, I want to change my look.

Well, we do a lot of Madonnas, he said.

Nah, gimmie a mohawk . . . and color it blue. *I* feel blue and I want my hairs to match.

A short time later she stood outside on Astor Place, a cool breeze playing on parts of her head she never knew existed before. Startled commuters on their way home from work stared at her. She felt good. It was nice to be noticed.

Next she went into a cheap boutique and bought a second-hand pair of black pants. A size too small. She dumped her old jeans in a wastebasket by the dressing room door. She also bought a black leather vest. It wiped out the last of her cash, but it had the neatest silver studs on the shoulders.

She had to go back to their tiny apartment to put on the final touch. I know *exactly* what I've got to do, she said out loud, Duke will be so proud of me. She took a half-finished bottle of whiskey from behind a stack of dirty dishes and polished it off. Then she took some ice cubes and a needle to the bathroom with her.

Leaning on the sink, she looked at herself in the mirror. It took a couple of moments to bring her reflection into focus. Then she quickly punched three holes in each side of her nose and inserted three different pairs of earrings. There was blood all over the place—tiny streams of red stained the sink—and droplets splattered onto the tiled floor.

Jill walked back over to Avenue A. There was a gaggle of punks hanging out in front of the Pyramid Club. Jill joined them. Nobody said a word.

She'd been accepted.

A BAD DAY

Duke knew it was going to be a bad day, even before he got out of bed. He had a splitting headache, and a lump the size of a nickel bag on the back of his neck. He couldn't remember where he'd been last night—or how he got home. Jill was nowhere around. She'd probably gone out to look for another part-time job.

Duke dragged himself into their tiny kitchen to get a bite to eat. But of course there wasn't a single bit of food in the house—which shouldn't have surprised him. There seldom was.

Fucking shit, he groaned, now I'm gonna have to go out.

He took the bike he'd 'borrowed' from a friend down six flights of steps to the street. He was sweating and cursing by the time he finally reached the ground floor. Duke aimed himself toward one of the cheap Ukranian coffee shops in the neighborhood and pedaled off. A bit unsteadily.

About five blocks from his building he smacked into a pothole. He saw it at the last moment and tried to swerve but a speeding New York Post delivery truck didn't give him any choice. He broke a couple of spokes and bent the front tire.

Fucking shit, he yelled. He righted the bike and started to walk it in the direction of the restaurant.

Well, my friend, a dude in a parka said to him, looks like you've got problems.

Yeah, Duke mumbled, noticing that the guy had a brown paper bag on the end of one arm.

I'd like to use your wheels for awhile, the dude said.

Go fuck yourself, Duke replies.

Hey, be cool, man. I got a gun in here, the guy said grinning. He gave Duke a flash of metal. And I want your cash, too.

It's yours, Duke said quickly, letting go of the bike.

The dude took his money and told him to split. Duke went back to his building, his stomach growling. He'd have to get some stuff to sell on the street to get some cash so he could eat. What a lousy day.

But it got worse. He got back just in time to see through the smashed door two guys ducking out a window with the few things of any value they had left. Duke was too wasted to give chase.

It took him a couple of hours to panhandle enough money to buy a new lock for the door and a sandwich. As he entered his building again a voice called out from behind the stairwell:

Stick em up.

Fucking *shit*, Duke said, I don't *have* anything. We just *got* robbed.

What's in the bag, the voice asked.

A new lock for our apartment and a sandwich, Duke replied.

That'll do just fine, the voice said, hand it over.

Can I at least keep the *sandwich*, Duke asked.

No, the voice answered.

DUKE & JILL BOTTOM-OUT

They made it almost to the Ohio border on Interstate 80 before their car broke down completely. It took them a couple of days to hitch back to the city. A friend let them crash in a tiny unused storeroom in a sixth-floor walkup.

Duke was feeling pretty discouraged by then. He had no money, no job, and no prospects of getting either in the near future.

Jill rallied and got a gig doing phone sales two days a week for a novelty company. She even figured out a way to get enough cash to get them through the week. She applied for an American Express card and got her boss to lie about her salary. She'd call around, using the phone at work, and find out which of her friends were about to go on a shopping spree—go to the store with them on her days off and charge their purchases on her card—and then get the cash later. Of course a scheme like that could only last so long. She was beginning to approach her credit limit.

Duke pitched in with a couple of ideas of his own. He collected beer bottles and soda cans from city trash baskets, and panhandled on the street. And every afternoon he'd sit on a worn blanket outside the Cooper Union Building and try to sell off the last of their possessions—his old platform shoes, Jill's beat-up spikes, some tattered paperbacks and a couple of well thumbed girlie magazines. He felt like a person from another era—like a ghost from the depression years—he'd seen pictures of them in the school library before he dropped out.

Duke kept hoping they'd be able to put together enough cash to swing another drug deal. But, realistically, he knew he'd have to figure out something else. The word was out, and no one in their right mind would take a chance on selling him anything. Someone was after them. Every day at noon a gray Mercedes would pull up in front of their building and sit there for half an hour or so, and then slowly drive away.

Jill was scared. She couldn't understand why Duke was treating the situation so lightly. But Duke had finally come up with a plan.

He made up a flyer announcing the availability of their space for sublet, and notched a row of tear slips with the telephone number of a pay-phone near his afternoon selling spot on the bottom. He xeroxed about fifty copies and posted them in health-food stores, coffee shops and in the neighborhood bookstore on St. Mark's Place. The response was immediate. He ended up getting one month's rent and security (which came to about $800) from seven different people. They all seemed very happy to give him their money—and Duke was equally happy to receive it.

Let's go get stoned, he said to Jill, as they walked west on East Fourth Street.

Hand of a Wanker

BY PATRICK McGRATH

BABYLONIA—ENTANKED IN THE ILL-LIT MOOD lounge of a nightclub called Babylonia, a sleek green lizard with a crest of fine spines and a bright ruff under its throat gazed unblinking into the glassy eyes of Lily de Villiers. Lily peered back and tapped the tank with a talonlike fingernail. On the couch beneath the video screen Dicky Dee languidly eyed young Gunther, who wore only purple lederhosen and had a magnificent physique. Dicky himself was in plastic sandals, khaki shorts, Hawaiian shirt and white pith helmet.

"Lily," he murmured.

The lizard didn't move, and nor did Lily.

"Lily."

"Oh what?"

"Fix me a drink, sweetie."

It was late afternoon, the club was empty and the bar was open. Lily straightened up and wobbled over on heels like needles. As she reached for the vodka Dicky's eyes wandered back to young Gunther's pectorals. Upstairs a telephone rang. The air conditioner was humming. It was summer, and no one was in town. Then Lily screamed.

"Oh good god, what is it?" exclaimed Dicky.

Lily was staring at something in the sink. She picked it up gingerly, then screamed again and flung it on the bar.

"It's real!" she cried.

"What is?" said Dicky, gazing at the ceiling.

"It's a—hand!"

A faint gleam appeared in Dicky Dee's eyes. "A hand?" he murmured, rising from the couch.

● ● ●

The mood lounge was a long room with a low ceiling and no windows. The bar occupied one end and there was a stuffed ostrich at the other. A few tables and chairs were scattered about the floor. In the permanent gloom one did not notice that the paint was peeling and the linoleum cracking; for usually the place was full of decadent types gossiping in blasé tones about drugs, love and disease. But this was the afternoon; it was summertime; and they were the only ones in there.

Dicky peered at the thing on the bar. It was indeed a hand. The skin was pale, with fine black, hairs on both back and palm, oddly enough. The blood on the stump was black and congealed, though the fingernails were nicely trimmed. Dicky looked from Lily to Gunther and back to the hand. Tittering slightly, he took the cigarette from his mouth and put it between the fingers.

"Oh Dicky!" cried Lily, turning away. "How could you? It might be someone we know."

"True," said Dicky, taking back his cigarette. "Anyway, you need a lung to smoke. Let's go and tell Yvonne. Maybe it's Yvonne's hand."

● ● ●

Yvonne was in charge of the bookings, and could be found in the office at this time of day. He was peering anxiously at a calendar covered with illegible scrawls and mumbling into a telephone squashed between ear and shoulder when Lily and Dicky entered the office. They could see immediately that both his hands were firmly attached to their wrists. He raised his eyes toward the ceiling, pressed his lips together, and pulled his mouth into a long sagging line of weary resignation. With his off-white mohawk tumbling in disarray about his ears, he looked, thought Dicky, rather like a sheep.

"I'm going to put you on hold, Tony," he said. "Something's come up." He hung up.

"Come downstairs, darling," said Dicky Dee. "You need a drink." Yvonne glanced at Lily's face. Why was the girl so pale? It was rather becoming. He rose from his desk like a man in pain and ran a thin bejewelled hand through his hair. "I think I do," he said. Down they went then, Yvonne and Dicky in front, and Lily tottering behind them.

● ● ●

But when they got to the lounge, the hand was gone.

"It's gone!" cried Dicky.

"What?" said Yvonne.

"There was a severed hand on the bar!"

Yvonne sighed, and began to make himself a drink. Dicky Dee turned to young Gunther, who was still sitting on the couch and flexing his Gothic pects.

"Gunther, what happened to the hand?" Dicky appeared rattled. He generated emotion.

Gunther shrugged.

"Hands don't just—disappear!" whispered Dicky, blanching.

Gunther shrugged again. Yvonne shrugged. Lily was looking under the bar, joggling the bottles. "Maybe it slipped down," she said. Then she screamed—for out of the darkness leaped the hand itself!

It scampered across the bar, hurled itself onto the floor and ran down the room and out of the door at the end. There was a moment of stunned silence and then Yvonne dropped his drink. It shattered messily on the floor.

"Mein gott," breathed Gunther. "The dead hand lives."

Dicky strode manfully toward the door. "I'm going after it," he said. Then he stopped, turned, and came back to the bar. "I think I need a little drink first," he said. "This is extremely fucking weird."

● ● ●

None of them mentioned what they'd seen. They sensed, rightly, that others would be skeptical; the staff of Babylonia had never been known for rigor in perceptual matters. Three nights later St. Mark and His Evangelists were playing the upstairs room. Toward the end of their late set St. Mark paused to catch his breath and introduce the next number.

"This one's called Witch Bitch," he grunted, fingering his iron cross. "Dedicated to my mother—"

Then he screamed.

The audience thought the scream was all part of it. The band knew it wasn't, and so did Dicky Dee. He'd seen the hand dropping from the ceiling, and he rushed for the stage as St. Mark staggered backwards into the drums, clawing at the thing clamped to his neck. The kids applauded with gusto as the skinny singer overturned a cymbal, and by the time Dicky got onstage the rest of the band was desperately attempting to pry the hand off St. Mark's throat. But the diabolical fingers could not be moved. St. Mark's face, meanwhile, had turned scarlet, his eyes were bulging, and his tongue protruded grotesquely from his throat. The applause had by this time turned to screams, but through it all Dicky could hear one clear voice:

"Burn it off! Burn it off!"

Of course! Dicky Dee lit a cigarette with trembling fingers and ground it into the back of the hand. It was a dramatically effective move. The hand immediately loosed its grip and scuttled under an upset drum—and not a moment too soon, as far as St. Mark was concerned. They helped him offstage, and by a stroke of good fortune there were stimulants on hand to help revive the half-choked performer. He was soon his old "self" again, apparently none the worse for his encounter with the hand.

"But where did it come from?" he said, gently fingering his long white stringy neck. No one could answer him. "What a grip," he said, in a tone of some respect. "Look at those bruises!" They looked at the bruises; and within an hour, a number of leading Babylonians were sporting on their necks cosmetic stranglemarks in exquisitely brutal shades of red, purple, and black.

Three days later Lily was tending bar upstairs when she noticed a rather unusual character enter the club. He stood close to the door, grinning wildly at nothing in particular as his eyes darted suspiciously from side to side. But what struck Lily as odd was this: when he paid for his Guinness, and she caught a glimpse of his palm—there were hairs growing on it! She was about to strike up a conversation on the topic when the tranquility of Babylonia was yet again shattered by a bloodcurdling scream. It came from the ladies' washroom—and a moment later a young woman came crashing through the door, still pulling up her fishnet tights.

"Fucking men!" she shouted. "You can't take a piss without being molested!" She collapsed onto a barstool, and to the small crowd of anxious drinkers that had quickly gathered round her she pointed with trembling finger into the washroom. "In there!" she cried.

"What, a man?" said Lily. It had happened before.

"No!" wailed the distressed girl. "A man's *hand*!"

Lily looked at Dicky, who had just emerged from the office, and Dicky dashed into the washroom. A moment later he came out again. "It's gone," he said.

"Back where it came from, I hope!" said the girl, with a shudder of deep distaste.

The story, as Dicky and Lily told it to Yvonne in the office a few minutes later, was that the hand had been lurking in the U-bend of the toilet upon which the unfortunate girl had seated herself, and the temptation, clearly, had been irresistible. When the girl had fled, shrieking, the hand had in all probability returned to the safety of the U-bend.

"So at least we know it's amphibious," murmured Yvonne.

"It's amphibious, cunning, murderous—and horny," said Dicky, pacing back and forth. "The question is—"

At that moment there was a loud rap at the door. "Go away!" shouted Yvonne. There was a moment's silence; then the rap came again.

"Go away!" shouted Yvonne and Lily. But the door opened, and there stood the black-clad stranger whom Lily had noticed earlier—the one with hair on the palm of his hand!

"Excuse me," he said in deep, hollow tones. There was a moment's silence; then Yvonne rose to his feet irritably.

"We're in a meeting," he grumbled. "Can't you—"

"The hand," said the stranger. "I can help you."

Yvonne stopped grumbling. Dicky looked up. "You can?" he said. "What do you know?"

"Can I come in?" said the stranger.

"Come in, come in," said Yvonne, pushing a chair forward. "Tell us what you know."

"Very well," said the stranger, seating himself and pulling out a pack of Marlboro. "Mind if I smoke?"

"Smoke, smoke," said Yvonne. "Just tell us about the hand, will you."

So the stranger told them about the hand.

THE CURSE OF HUMAN DESIRE

The stranger accepted a light from Yvonne, drew heavily on his cigarette, and stared at the floor. At last he lifted his eyes—tormented, bloodshot eyes, filmed with despair—and Lily felt a small gush of pity for the man. There were deep bags under his eyes, and his skin was unnaturally pale. "You see before you," he said at last, in those hollow tones of his, "a victim of human desire. Not a pretty sight, is it?" There was another pause. Yvonne cleared his voice and said: "Who—"

"Oh, my name doesn't matter," said the stranger. "I am just one of many, a ruined man, ruined by... " Here he was unable to finish his sentence; a sob wracked his frame.

"Human desire?" said Dicky.

"Exactly!" said the stranger. "Everywhere I look I see lips, breasts, bottoms, legs—and I've had enough! I can't stand it anymore—this constant itch—this *compulsion*! I'm a sick man!" he cried—and then his voice dropped an octave, or more. "I'm a compulsive masturbator, you see," he whispered. "I have to wank. And this"—he slowly opened his hand—"is the result." It was then that Dicky and Yvonne saw what Lily had seen earlier: dead in the center of his palm sprouted a small clump of fine black hairs!

"Just like an armpit," murmured Yvonne. "Go on."

"It all began," continued the stranger, "with the onset of puberty. Slowly it took over my life. I couldn't escape, it was like a machine, constantly filling my head with these—images!" He shuddered. "I lost my job. Dishonorable discharge. Ha! Story of my life... " There was a long silence. Then, lifting his eyes, the stranger cried out in anguish: "How long can a man live with shame?"

Dicky looked at Yvonne. Yvonne shrugged. "We don't know," he said. "How long?"

"Only so long!" the stranger cried, and suddenly rising to his feet he pulled from his pocket, where it had been tucked since the beginning of the interview, his right hand—only there was no right hand! He hauled up his sleeve to show how the wrist ended in a smooth, round, dimpled stump. Wordlessly the three Babylonians gazed at the stranger's stump. They'd not met a story like this one before, and Lily slipped out to get them all a drink.

"You can still do it with your left one, I suppose?" said Yvonne.

"Masturbation guilt drove me to it," said the stranger, resuming his seat. "Yes, masturbation guilt! I hacked it off myself, and I should have drowned it, I suppose, but I couldn't bring myself to do it..." There was a pregnant silence. "I come from a sentimental race, you see," he went on. "I put it in a shoe box and kept it under the sink instead."

"A shoe box," said Lily, who had returned with drinks. "Cute."

"Oh, there were holes in it," said the stranger, taking a long swallow of his Guinness. "But anyway, for a week I wasn't troubled by the curse of human desire—yes, for the first time since puberty. I didn't feel the itch! Can you imagine it—a world without breasts, without skin, without bums and lips and legs...a world free of desire, where everything is what it seems and your brain isn't polluted with longing and your loins aren't constantly stirring with a life of their own...can you imagine what it is to be free of human desire?"

They all nodded.

"It couldn't last. It returned in the depths of the night, as I slept. I felt it creep under the blankets. I felt its fingers on my thigh, soft as silk. I felt it gently laying hold of me—and I rose up from my bed with a shout and I *hurled* the thing from me! Oh, I couldn't have it starting again, not after all I'd been through! 'Back to your box!' I shouted—and to see it drag itself out of the door and into the kitchen—it was a pathetic sight, so it was. But I had to be firm, you see that?"

They all nodded.

"I never saw it again," said the stranger. There was a long pause. A muted roar of conversation was audible from the bar beyond. At last Dicky spoke. "And you think it's your hand that's been causing trouble here?" he said

"I do," said the stranger, who had finished his Guinness and pulled out another cigarette. "I was in here the night before—before I cut it off. I think it remembers. I think it came back." He clutched his face in his hand. "Oh god," he sobbed, "if only I'd been strong. If only I'd flushed it down the toilet in the beginning—"

"It wouldn't have done any good," Dicky cut in. "It's amphibious."

"No!" said the stranger.

"But more to the point," said Dicky, "how can we catch it?"

"Oh, I'll tell you how to catch it," said the stranger, "and I'll tell you what to do with it once you've caught it." And he pulled from inside his coat a hefty meat cleaver—the very same one, he told them, he'd used on the hand in the first place. And then he outlined his plan . . .

DER TOD UND DIE HAND

Late that night—very late, when the club had emptied and everyone had
gone home to bed—or to the after-hours place on Avenue B—Lily de Villiers
sat alone in the ill-lit mood lounge of Babylonia. Lily was looking her best. Her
red hair was piled up on top with thick strands curling saucily down around her
face and throat. Her eyes were heavily mascaraed and her lips were scarlet.
Rouge highlights on her cheeks created an impression of mounting inner passion. She was in deep décolletage, her cleavage shadow sharply accentuated by
the subdued lighting of the mood lounge, and her little leather skirt riding high
up thighs sheathed in sleek black seamed nylon stockings with runs and lad-
ders and other tarty insignia. Her legs were crossed and her heels, as ever, were
like needles. She was heavily perfumed. She exuded availability. She was the
whore of Babylonia, and she was there to bait the hand.

An hour passed, and Lily sat smoking cigarettes and pouting provocatively.
She crossed and recrossed her legs every few minutes, and the ashtray on the
couch beside her gradually filled to overflowing. Lily got to her feet and, unsure what strange eye might be watching, tottered sexily over to the bar and
emptied the ashtray into a garbage can. Then she returned to the couch and
resumed sitting, smoking, pouting, waiting, and crossing and recrossing her
legs.

Another hour passed. Poor Lily was starting to yawn. The sun was coming up.
Honest citizens were going to work. She was about to call it a night and go
upstairs to the others when a tiny sound caught her attention. Could it be? It
could—someone—or something—was coming down the stairs!

Lily smoked with a careless nonchalance honed to perfection by years of
practice. She was very cool. And there it was!—pattering across the floor like
some hideous pink crab, slapping the linoleum as it scampered toward her in
lusty and intemperate haste. From fifteen feet it hurled itself upon her, groping
like a maniac at her bosom! Lily rose into the air with a wild shriek of horror,
and toppled backwards as from beneath the couch reared young Gunther, who
had been waiting there all the while, and who now brandished aloft the stranger's meat cleaver! Lily seized the hand clamped to her bosom and plucked it
loose like a limpet from a rock and hurled it with a cry of disgust against the
wall. The hand fell, stunned, to the floor, and lay on its back, its white, tender,
hairy underside exposed to the fierce lunge of the young German. Then down
came the cleaver and mercilessly hacked the dazed hand in two! The shattered
and bleeding half-hands lurched off in opposite directions, but far too shakily
to escape Gunther's terrible wrath. Slash slash! Down came the cleaver twice
more, and the hand was severed in four. From four to eight and from eight to
sixteen; and when the cursed creature that had spilled the stranger's seed so

needlessly all those years was finally reduced to somewhere in the region of fifty parts, and none of them was moving, Gunther stopped. He mopped his brow and lifted his head, his breast damp and heaving, to the light, which Dicky Dee had just flicked on.

"Good work, Gunther," said Dicky, his eyes burning with a morbid and unnatural gleam. "And Lily"—he went to the poor girl, who was rising unsteadily to her feet after gazing aghast at Gunther's grunty choppings; "my poor dear Lily. A hero!"

"Heroine," gasped Lily.

"Heroine," cried Dicky.

"Heroine," murmured Yvonne, entering.

"Heroine!" thundered Gunther, brandishing the bloody cleaver.

At that moment the stranger's hollow tones were heard. "The hand is dead," he said, pausing in the doorway. "Feed it to the lizard. Long live the hand!" And with a dry bitter laugh—or was it just a bad cough, a dirty hack spawned of some putrid existential miasma that seethed within his guilt-ridden soul?—anyway, with a sound that chilled the racing, roaring blood of the four young people, the stranger waved his stump over his head and limped off into the sharp Manhattan dawn.

The Dog-Eater

BY JORGE CABALQUINTO

t was the piss on the snow
On a sidewalk in New York
That brought up the thought of a moon
In his childhood: in a cloudless sky,
A clean sphere like a huge new lamp
Under which, for the first time, the boy saw the dog-eater.

It was said in the barrio of San Miguel that the man Jose
Ate dog's meat each day of the week
And the village dogs could tell this from his scent,
That eating dog's meat occasionally was all right
But to do it every day makes you smell like a dog yourself.
But they said Jose knew that too and he was a man
Who knew who he was and what he was doing.

On the moon-lit night he saw the dog-eater
He heard the barking and howling, first from a distance
Softly, then rising in volume like an accompaniment
To something coming that was dangerous to someone—
Though not to the boy who eagerly waited.

He saw him from the window of his house:
A small dark man in a dark shirt who walked
Easily, as if oblivious to the noise and commotion
That followed him, as all the dogs in all the houses
(All houses in the boy's village had dogs
And the boy's house had three) came out
To complain, barking and following the dog-eater
Though they dared not come close enough to do him any harm.

The dog-eater, the light of the moon on his white hair
And on his thin clothes, walked by with his head tilted
To the ground. He never lifted his head
Even when somebody called out his name
And said something the boy did not understand.
He kept his eyes to the gravel road, walking
Until his body disappeared at the bend.

When the dog-eater was gone the boy looked up:
He saw again the bright moon in the cloudless sky.
He stared at its huge and pervasive presence—
Its color like the color that many years later
He would see on a patch of snow
On a sidewalk in New York.

Venus

BY JOSHUA WHALEN

 FIRST MET CAROLINE IN THE SUMMER OF 1983, A FEW weeks after I returned to New York and the East Village from Seattle.

It was a very brief encounter, that first time on the stairs in that tenement on East Tenth Street. I was helping a friend carry some heavy boxes up to their apartment, she was hurrying down them, taking the steps two at a time, late for work. She wore the standard black leather motorcycle jacket, with a white button-down shirt and worn Levi's. Trying to look like Patti Smith, only she was too pretty. She had long reddish brown hair and green eyes, and soft Celtic features with pronounced cheek bones. I was twenty years old that year, and she couldn't have been even that. She tossed off a quick "Hi!" as she squeezed past us on the stairs and then was gone.

It's considered not only naive, but downright cliché to suggest that anyone can fall in love from just one such encounter, but I've always believed that was how it was with us. The second time we met was in a bar on St. Marks Place which has long since been overrun and subsequently abandoned by NYU students, but at the time was a well-kept secret known only known only to an adventurous few. It was Martilaina who introduced us. I'd wandered in after midnight and she and Caroline had been sitting together in a booth with empty bottles neatly lined up along the edge of the table and half-empty bottles in front of them. I'd walked up to them and said hello. Martalaina smiled and turned to Caroline and said, "This is Jay, he grew up down here" as if that was all there was to it. Regardless, it was the right introduction because Caroline lit up and I sat down and the rest of the night she couldn't get enough, virtually interrogated me, asking questions and not even waiting for answers. She'd grown up in Wyoming, in the middle of nowhere, and dreamed and schemed of going anywhere, anywhere else at all, but especially here, the place she'd read about in novels and seen in movies and heard about in songs. Everyone in Wyoming thought she was nuts. I told her Wyoming was a good place to have left. She liked that. A few months later we moved in together.

Caroline fancied herself a poet. She moved in that fall with a carload of books and her Sears electric portable. She had a job at an after-hours club on Clinton Street, and I was working at the 8BC theater on East 8th Street. We would get up at three in the afternoon and eat dinner of a sort, then soak ourselves in coffee and go to our respective appointments with responsibility. At dawn we'd meet at Leshko's on 7th and A and eat breakfast, replenish the caffeine in our blood-streams, and then go home and get into bed.

On beautiful Sundays that we both had the night off we'd wake even later. Even after living together since mid-September—and here it was November—we still had not run out of things to talk about. I'd tell stories of having seen concerts of the Who or Jimi Hendrix at the Filmore when I was only six years old, of periodic trips upstate to Woodstock to try (unsuccessfully) to get child support payments out of my ever-absent father, of living in a Brooklyn ghetto after that because mom couldn't make ends meet in the East Village and so we'd moved in with my grandparents. She would talk about Wyoming, of how the only people who ever used the library in Cheyenne had been winos and old people, how everyone had thought her crazy for talking about wanting to leave. She would get nervous and tense when she brought up her parents' nearly having her committed when they caught her smoking pot at fourteen, or how her Pentecostal father had finally driven her out on her own at fifteen with his vituperations about sin and hellfire, and the vengeance of the lord. Now and then she'd read me something she'd written, cautiously searching my face for approval or criticism, uttering her voices in the sing-song rhythm of a Baptist minister. We could have gone on like that forever, but then something changed.

It was around New Years that it started. Suddenly, the easiness and comfortable decay that had been the hallmarks of the Lower East Side began to change. Caroline didn't meet me at Leshko's one morning. I went down to Clinton Street to look for her and found the club swarming with cops, the owner being led off in handcuffs. Caroline was pleading desperately with a plainclothes man. He kept shaking his head. Finally he turned around and walked away from her, ignoring her as she shouted after him. That was only the beginning.

All that winter it felt as if we were living in occupied territory. Every street from Delancey to 14th was flooded with cops of every description. Systematically, a block, sometimes only a building at a time, they swept through the slum, securing territory, ostensibly to wipe out the drug traffic that had prospered for almost two decades in the battered tenements, abandoned, fire-gutted shells, and garbage-strewn lots. However that may have been, whatever their alleged intent, in their wake fell every after-hours club, every seedy bar, every street peddler, every graffiti artist. People no longer congregated on stoops, or even on street corners, afraid of being locked up in central booking for a week while the police ran an identity check. I was stunned, horrified. Before my very eyes what amounted to the only heritage I had was being wiped out as surely as if there had been a right-wing military coup, which perhaps there had been. If I was stunned, however, Caroline, who had only arrived a year earlier, was shattered. The vengeance of the lord had descended.

The after-hours club on Clinton Street never reopened after it was shut down for not having a license. Caroline hadn't gotten another job, and now we were living entirely on my hundred and twenty dollars a week. She would sit in her chair in the kitchen, at her desk by the window, in front of her typewriter, staring out into the airshaft and rocking back and forth like an autistic child. Now and then we'd try to talk, but things had changed. There wasn't a beautiful magical village of random factors outside our door anymore. There was only Prague, or Chile.

For a while things continued to follow the established routine, but without any life, like a robot carrying out its last instructions endlessly, because it doesn't know what else to do. I still went to work at five, and came home at four. Caroline would be sitting up waiting for me, the books of her adolescence scattered around the bedroom floor as she pored over them endlessly, and sometimes cried. She fled from paperback to paperback, looking for who knows what, some small comfort, anything but watching her life's desire vivisected before her eyes and reassembled into a shopping mall. The typewriter stood gathering dust in the kitchen, while her mind burned with her father's last words to her, the last time they spoke, when she was just fifteen, that she would come to no good.

At six a.m. we went to breakfast like always. Greasy eggs and potatoes. She smiles a little, and as we leave, she looks up into the early morning twilight, sees the lone star shining there and whispers, mistakenly, "Venus."

A week later she left. I don't know where, and no one has heard from her since. I came home one day and she was gone, and just a note, just goodbye, and nothing else, all her clothes gone and the typewriter. All she left were the books. I guess she just didn't want them anymore.

I stayed in that apartment for another month or two, but it was like living in an empty cathedral. The ceiling hung over me, the windows admitted their dust-filtered smudges of sunlight, and nothing made a sound except the pipes in the walls, vainly pumping steam into the icy vacuum that was all that remained.

I stayed in that apartment for another month or two, but the ceiling hung over me, the windows admitted their dust-filtered smudges of sunlight, and nothing made a sound except the pipes in the walls, vainly pumping steam into the icy vacuum that was all that remained.

Between a Dream and a Cup of Coffee

BY PETER CHERCHES

THE DREAM—I WENT TO A SHOE STORE and bought a new pair of sneakers. My old shoes were in wretched shape, so I threw them out and wore the sneakers. I had the receipt in my hand when I left the store, and I looked at it. I won't need this for anything, I thought, so I tore it up and threw it away. Then I started walking. I walked for a long time, but I had no idea where I was going. I walked what seemed like hundreds of city blocks, some familiar, some not. After a while I noticed a problem with my sneakers: the stitching was coming un-done—my new shoes were falling apart at the seams. I was distressed. I didn't know what to do. Perhaps I should return them and get a new pair, I thought. Then I remembered that I had thrown the receipt away. Now I couldn't return the shoes. And I couldn't go any further because my shoes were falling apart. I was stuck.

● ● ●

I woke up thinking about the events of the day before. It had been a particularly odd day. First there was that crazy woman. And then that thing in the bank. And then the incident at the supermarket.

THE WOMAN

The lines at Unemployment were longer than usual that day, and it took three hours just to sign. When I finally got out all I wanted to do was get home and take a quick nap. But first I had to go to the bank and get some cash. And I had to go to the supermarket to stock up on essentials. So I was on my way to the bank when this thing happened. An old lady, whom I had never seen before, came up to me and said she was my mother. She grabbed my arm and said, "Sonny, I've found you!"

"What are you talking about?" I said, wresting my arm from her grip.

"Sonny, I've found you!" she repeated.

"Who are you and what do you want with me?" I asked.

"I'm your mother, Sonny, don't you remember?"

"My mother is dead," I told her.

She began to cry. "Sonny, you're breaking my heart," she said.

She was making me nervous. "Look, lady," I said, "I'm very busy and I've got to get going."

"Why are you doing this to me," she asked, still crying.

"I don't know what you're talking about," I said.

"I've been searching for you all these years—ever since you left me. And I've finally found you. Please come home with me."

She wanted me to go home with her.

I went home with her.

Basically, I was interested by this point. I wanted to see what it was all leading to. So we took a cab to her house. It was a big house, and I got the impression that she was pretty well off. It started me thinking. I'm on unemployment—it sure would be nice not to pay rent anymore.

But I couldn't go through with it.

"Look," I said, "I'm not your son, so there's no use in my staying here." And I started walking toward the door.

She was crying.

THE BANK

So I went to the bank and another strange thing happened. I was standing on line and I saw a woman almost get her hand chewed off by the automatic teller. She had stuck her hand into the mouthlike drawer that delivers the money, to withdraw her cash, and the thing closed up with her hand in it. She tried to yank her hand out, but the thing was closed too tight. A couple of people ran over to help and tried to pry the drawer open, but it wouldn't budge. Finally, someone on line figured out how she could get her hand out: all she had to do was request more cash, and when the drawer opened up again she could remove her hand. So she pushed the button for another twenty with her free hand, entered her secret code, put her card in the slot, and when the thing opened up she withdrew her hand and her cash. Her wrist was throbbing and swelling. Tears were streaming down her cheeks. She picked up the customer service phone and started screaming at them, threatening to sue, and they told her she would have to put a formal complaint in writing. I wondered whether it was her writing hand that had been caught.

Anyway, when my turn came I took out fifty and then I headed for the supermarket.

THE SUPERMARKET

I don't like supermarkets, but they're cheaper than bodegas, so I go to them when I have to stock up on essentials. But they always have the air conditioning up too high, they're always playing muzak, and you're always bumping into people in the aisles. And this time, to add insult to injury, there was the thing with the nickels.

I had brought my groceries, mostly paper goods, to the chekout. The cashier tallied my items and the total came to nineteen-forty. I gave her a twenty and she gave me my change—twelve nickels. Would you believe it—twelve nickels! I couldn't believe it. You just don't do that with nickels. You don't go handing them out in bulk. It's not right. Nickels are too big. They're a necessary evil when it comes to small change, like to account for a five-cent denomination, but a whole bunch all at once? That's inexcusable. Nickels are big coins. Much too big when you consider what they're worth: five cents. Five lousy cents! A dime is worth ten cents and it's a lot smaller than a nickel. Dimes make sense, nickels don't. I'd guess that, speaking purely in terms of size, a nickel is roughly three times the size of a dime. Now does that seem right? A dime is worth twice as much as a nickel, yet in the same amount of pocket space it takes to carry around a nickel you can carry three dimes, which comes out to thirty cents. That's simple arithmetic. Or take a quarter. A quarter looks bigger than a nickel, but I'd say it's not really that much bigger because it's thinner. And besides, a quarter's worth twenty-five cents, so you can't complain about a quarter. But you can complain about nickels, and I did.

"What's the big idea, you giving me twelve nickels?" I said to the cashier. "Is this some kind of joke?"

"No sir," she said, "it's no joke. Your change was sixty cents. We had a surplus of nickels, and the manager told me I should give out as many nickels as possible."

"Well your surplus isn't my problem," I said, "so how about you giving me two quarters and a dime." I gave her the twelve nickels back.

She gave me two quarters and a dime. "I'm sorry, sir," she said. "No harm was intended."

I nodded my head and pocketed the change. It felt right. Two quarters and a dime. Without a doubt the best way to make sixty cents.

● ● ●

I was thinking about the nickel incident when I heard a knock at my door. I jumped out of bed, threw on some pants, and answered the door. It was a salesman.

THE SALESMAN

"Are you the head of this household?" the salesman asked.

"I am this household," I said.

"I'm selling light bulbs made by blind Chicano women, Christmas cards drawn by retarded children, and vacuum cleaners made by Aryan supermen."

"I don't have any discretionary income this week," I said.

"We have a lay-away plan."

"I'm not interested."

"Would you like a free dirt test?"

"What's that?" I asked.

He told me. "First I drop dirt all over your floor. Then I screw in one of these light bulbs, so you can see how dirty your floor is. Then I vacuum the floor—you'll be amazed at how clean it gets."

"I'm not interested," I said.

"Would you like to take a look at the Christmas cards?" he asked.

"I don't send Christmas cards," I said.

He picked up his stuff and knocked on the door across the hall. I closed my door.

I was ready to make my morning coffee, but when I looked in the fridge I discovered that I was all out of milk. I hate to drink my coffee black, so I had to go downstairs to the bodega to pick up a quart of milk.

THE VOICE ON THE PHONE

I picked up the phone to call the weather, to find out which coat I should wear, but there was no dial tone. Then I heard a voice. "Hello?"

"Hello," I said.

"Hello?"

I recognized the voice. It was a friend.

"Yeah, I'm here," I said.

"Oh. It didn't ring. I didn't hear any ringing on my end."

"I picked it up to make a call."

"Oh."

"Yeah, but you were there."

"Yeah, I called you."

"Yeah, I know."

"Yeah, I called you to find something out."

"Yeah? What's that?"

"I wanted to get your sister's number."

"I don't have a sister."

"Oh."

"Yeah. So why did you really call?"

"I needed someone to talk to."

"Me?"

"Yeah."

"You got a problem or something?"

"Nah."

"So what do you want to talk about?"

"Politics, baseball, food—anything."

"I was just on my way out."

"Yeah?"

"Yeah."

"That's okay."

"Yeah. So how about if I call you later?"

"Sure. That's okay."

"Okay, bye."

"Bye."

A WRONG NUMBER

I decided on a coat without calling the weather. I was just going downstairs anyway. I was on my way out when the phone rang. I picked it up. "Hello?"

"Hello, is Ralph there?"

"No," I said, "this isn't his number any more. It hasn't been for years."

I'm always getting these wrong numbers. Except it's the right number. That is, these people are calling *my* number, on purpose, for someone else. Always the same guy. Ralph. It's been happening ever since I moved in here. Ten years ago. At least once a month. I pick up the phone and someone says, "Hello, is Ralph there?"

The first couple of times, ten years ago, I figured it was just routine wrong numbers. Something close to mine, like maybe one digit off. But then I started asking. I said, "What number are you calling?" And they'd always give my number.

Ten years, and it still happens at least once a month. At first I figured maybe Ralph used to live here before me. I'd imagine this guy in my apartment, picking up the phone. Then I realized that he probably didn't live here at all. They rotate phone numbers. Ralph lived somewhere else, but he had my number.

Sometimes they think I'm Ralph. "Hey Ralphie, how ya doin'?"

All these people, all trying to get Ralph after all these years.

Ten years, at least one of these calls a month. That's at least 120 calls for Ralph. Probably more, because the calls were more frequent at the beginning. Maybe more like 150-175 calls. And I don't think any of them are repeaters, because I always explain that Ralph doesn't have this number anymore.

That's an awful lot of people.

Where is Ralph? Who is Ralph?

THE BODEGA

I finally got down to the bodega, but they were all out of quarts of milk. They did have pints, though. But pints were 45 cents and quarts were 60 cents. Two pints would give me a quart, but it would cost me 90 cents. One pint would do for the time being, of course, but then I'd have to buy another pint when I was done, and it would start a vicious cycle of pint buying. I'd be wasting loads of money if I kept buying pints. I *could* buy two pints now, just this once, and then start buying quarts again when I was done with the two pints, but I still didn't want to spend 90 cents for a quart when I could get one for 60. But I couldn't get a quart for 60 cents, because they were all out. Unless I went somewhere else. But I didn't want to go somewhere else because the next closest place was too far. So I stood there for a while, not knowing what to do. Finally, I decided not to buy any milk. I went back upstairs and had my coffee black.

52 ELENA'S RESTAURANT
SANDWICHES
COMIDAS
Coffee & Cake
CUCHIFRITOS
Y
FRITURAS

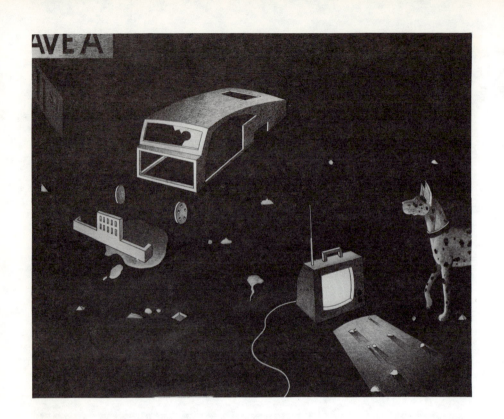

Auto da Fé

BY CARLE GROOME

THE DAY THE CAR CAME TO STAY WAS NOT ANY-thing to write home about.

They were out on the veranda, the steel beach that is, of their fourth-floor, streetfront walk-up. Not a breath inside, except for the rodent races occurring nightly under the floorboard speedway. So they opted for a little tanning and a lot of sobering up. And he rolls over to take a bit of bake on the back and sees the young woman wheeling the car to the terminal curb, steering from outside, propelled by a workforce of laughing homeboys at the bumpers and door handles.

"What's going on, love?" she asks without rolling over.

"Another little minidrama slipped out of life's endless motorcade, I suspect." The driver, having gone in for the keys, slammed the door of the sedan and kicked it several times before walking off in a towering snit. It sort of reminded him of how she'd been at the party the previous evening when he, a tad too much into his cups (as usual), had to be carried out to the car service. The nature of his fondness for the drink (and other excesses of character) being something of a running joke around their set, everyone had a good giggle about his performance. But it was no laughing matter later, and not much of a performance either. As a result, the heat was as stifling as the silence between them.

The next time he turned again, hours later, the scene had changed. Above, they were up to a bit of kissy-face and applying the grease to each other's extremities. Below, there was activity, a sort of deconstruction going on. The driverlady had pulled up in a van with a small press-gang of able-bodied Jamaicans. While one Rasta nattered about under the hood another was busy removing the plates as a third got the jack and the spare from the trunk. The engine contributed the battery and ignition coil, and probably the numbers off the block itself.

"It looks like we're going to have a visitor," he ventured, lifting his shades for emphasis.

"Do you think it's stolen?" She slid over his back, both groaning pleasantly at the slickness.

"Doubt it, darlin'," he drawled. "Anyways, flotsam or jetsam, it doesn't matter at this point... It's sheer abandonment now."

"HA!" She lifted her shades for emphasis and caught his attention up sharp. "Let's go back inside and I'll show you some 'sheer abandon'!"

Like the bent twig or the farmer's plow, there was a change in the street scene as the car began to alter its contours, adapting to the ecosystem, the lifestyle. By now the sweepers were making dirt furrows around this rock in the road. It blended in whith the grimy shade from the construction awning flanking the derelict building it stood beside. Some nights he would watch the junk trade stash their wares in its wheelbase, visiting its side with all the care and constancy of a well-paid R.N. on a deathwatch. Sometimes, when he'd have to go down to the storefront social club the dealers used as their HQ next door, to complain about the noise, he'd almost want to go over to the car. He had a vague impulse that if he could just bring himself to look inside, he might find out something about its past life... or how it was responding to its present one.

When he'd asked Super J to go get CBS, the chief, of a sorts, the car was supporting a beat box the size of a small steamer trunk, its dealer lounging about in the absence of any law.

"S'up, m'man?" CBS, a.k.a. Santana, lean, rangy and handsome in a Reuben Blades fashion, squatted beside him and stared at the car also.

"That guy one of your crew?"

"'S'it to you?" CBS smiled, taking the edge off his sharp tone. "You want to hire him or somethin'?"

"Maybe, But not as a D.J. It's kinda late, y'know. Maybe you could get him to cut the volume some. My girl and I could use a little peace. You got your business and it's none of mine. I stay out of yours, maybe you could keep yours out of my windows. OK?" They'd come to an understanding he and CBS, some time before when, in a drunken, drugged rage, he'd come leaping down the landings with a pool cue in his hand and started scaring the customers away, oblivious to the danger to himself. It was then that CBS had come out to tell him if he had any more problems to just come and see him first. The respect of territory; a pact between equals on either side of the insanity borderline.

CBS stood up, framed in the blue light that spilled out of the club's doorway. "YO! TURN THAT DOWN, MAN! PEOPLE TRYIN' TO GET SOME SLEEP!" The jams across the pavement were immediately halved. "Anythin' else I can do for you?" CBS smiled that charm again.

"Not unless you can tell me how to deal with my female troubles." He stood too, putting out a hand to shake with CBS.

CBS laughed a short snort. "HA! If I knew that I'd be an uptown head-doctor or a player. Jus' love 'em when you can and forget 'em the rest of the time. My daddy used to say a twist-up coathanger was pretty good 'tweentimes!" They released each other's grip and went their separate ways.

Back on the fire escape, he'd been sitting for hours with the cocktail shaker and the water pipe in easy reach, trying to reach a state of numbed nirvana while she studied for mid-terms. He'd been giving a lot of thought to the separate-but-equal status of his relationship with everything, and everyone around him. It was a convenient excuse for their sleeping arrangements as well. His night job made this petite "happy hour" a mellowing moment before the word processing detail later. After her temp work days and night classes there wasn't much of a morning for them either. Not that it made any difference to their lovelife; the last time they'd tried a 69 it ended up as a 96 and that 86'ed it for the past few weeks.

So it was somewhere beyond the third martini-&-bowl when he saw the answer, and, as it happened, it was the auto that authored the idea. He'd had a few swipes at the easel, unsatisfied with color or line in his mind, before chucking it in for the realism beyond the sash and the fantasy that tempted him from the bottle and the bag. Down at the curb a dominoes game continued unabated by the hawkers and addicts, the insect rattle of the tiles blending in with the hip-hop scratching, salsa and sirens. But over and above that was the clank and clatter of metal-on-metal sound that once more drew his attention from the stars and spheres of the sky back to his catbird seat over the street.

The hood of the car was open again and a wrecker's pick-up/tow truck had pulled up parallel. As he watched the surgeons he could see more vital organs yielded up to the suppliers' inventory: carburetor, radiator, fan, pistons, cam assembly... These were *real* mechanics, he thought, real salvage men. Not afraid to get deep into things to find what is valuable. And where was CBS' man tonight? Kind of early to run out of supplies...

Salvage. Take the parts out and see if they'll work in another setting. Recreation and re-creation. One is play and the other is to make anew. He liked the sound and the feel of it. All one needs to start over again is fresh supplies. Somehow it all seemed to fit.

"Hey love," he called from the sill. "What about a vacation to check the old inventory?"

"What? Did you say something?'

He raised his voice this time, just enough to get it across the intervening space. "I was saying let's take a trip and slough the slum. A weekend in Puerto Rico, maybe? It's only a couple hundred fare and board."

She came out of her study trance and walked over to lean on the kitchen jamb. "Are you serious? A weekend away from the Loisaidans to hang out with more of the same?" At least she was smiling now.

"Orlando then. Or the Poconos. Catskills. Virginia Beach. Some holiday place for lovers. A little good weather, a lot of romance, and some prime time sex. We can do repairs on this relationship…it only needs a bit of tuning. We just can't let it go to waste."

She went and sat on the radiator beside the sash. They faced each other as if on a love seat, perched between fear and hope with only the shaker and the pipe separating them. And she carefully removed even these obstacles. "Darling, I'm just as willing as you. I want to close this distance." She moved her face scant inches from his. "I want us to be just like this: body and soul."

He didn't even notice the cries of joy as the mechanics removed the oil pump.

By the time they'd returned, all lovey-dovey and blind to the world, it would be days before he noticed the car was up on blocks with only one tire remaining. It didn't take them long after to notice the dealers had moved into the building and had set up shop on the second floor landing.

At ground level he'd begun to informally chart the way the junker level would rise and fall, like tides, like the change of seasons, molting birds, or deciduous trees. There were the most amazing non-coincidences such as the beige, '73 Dodge Colt being parked behind another beige, '73 Dodge Colt as parts were transferred from the latter to the former. One stayed; the other didn't. It was simply a matter of shopping around for the right supplier. His street was one that accomodated long-term parking. Tow-trucks of the city rarely visited and the police had more important business than scofflaws. Lately, that interest had become one of accumulating the boiler plate steel doors that the members of the drug trade had installed in their various haunts, for security purposes. On those days a huge, municipal diesel would do a slow sweep of the neighborhood, the big crane in back gonging the heavy metal into its bin. The junkers would leave much less regularly. They just sat and quietly continued to oxidize: first, a bright orange as the paint flaked away from the winter's salt; then to a brownish earth tone as the natural grime and soot entered their pores; and finally, beginning to blend in with the gradations of gray exhaust that rose up from the tarmacadam.

He rubbed at the increasing stubble on his chin, now. Since leaving a state of regular employ shaving held less and less importance to him. She wasn't even complaining that it scratched her chin anymore. Their brief honeymoon passion had passed back to a peck on the cheek before the door and just another before the pillow. It was getting harder to see her as the credit hours marched on and his temp hours were extended to earn a little extra in private enterprise. So he only rubbed at the stubble and looked up at the lights of the apartment, mildly curious what subject she might be studying then.

The coarseness of his face contrasted with the smoothness of his musings. He'd no reason to interrupt her, and he had two friends to help pass the time: Jack Daniels and the visitor. Snuggling into the slope of the hood and the mouth of the half-pint, he felt only the ease of the evening; the warmth of the metal in the dusk and the false heat of the bourbon burning inside. The all-around glow of these effects lulled him into a thermonuclear nod. He dreamed of being behind the wheel with his girl at his side and a wide, open highway, driving into a golden horizon. Whether a sunrise or sunset, it wasn't clear. Maybe the valium was kicking in too.

As the mercury lamps bathed him and the vehicle in a lurid yellow patina, he rolled over and stared into the innards for the first time. Beyond the rearview mirror and its deodorant pine tree, the bucket seats were gone. The stick removed and the steering wheel bent. The dash gutted and stripped, loose wires dangling over shattered plastic. With his forehead mashed to the glass he could see the building reflected, the lights of their rooms had gone out now. The world had dimmed around his dream.

He was still pondering 'recreation and recreation' when the new doorman asked for his tracks. He thought about the tracks a car makes and the roads we all must travel down; he thought about telling him to shove it; he thought about suicide . . . all at once.

"Tenant," he muttered as they slid open the double dead-bolts to leat him into his home.

She was still up with the phone, just cradling it when he walked in. "Now they've got one in our building." Her voice was calm; somewhere near the precipice of hysteria, yet calm. "This is just too much. I feel like a prisoner in my own home."

He sat opposte her at the kitchen table. He wanted to explain the evolutionary process of junkies and the ecosystem of junkers and tie it all up so she could accept it with the same appreciation of the grand order of things that he did. He wanted to hold her in his arms and tell her that everything was all right. He wanted to lead a ghetto pogrom. He didn't. He couldn't. He didn't bother.

He closed the windows against the noise outside and saw someone shooting up in the back seat of the car.

CBS explained it as purely a safety move. "We got problems with them boys up the block. You know them, 'The Killers,' 'Brown Door'?"

"I've seen them. I usually avoid walking that way. They're rude to my girlfriend. Even some of your guys . . . "

"Hey, you got any trouble with them I'll pass the word. No problem!" CBS always wore a big brass buckle with the three letters standing out about that many inches high. He wondered if it would be impertinence to ask if those were his real initials or whether he just liked TV a lot. He didn't want to press these few concessions. He no longer had the insane rages to lash out at them; it took too much energy to get his anger out of his mind, let alone the door. He wondered when he'd lost the upper hand with them. Was it the first time he requested something rather than demanded it? Did it matter? He hoped they thought of him as a tame lion, but he suspected it was probably a much lesser cat. 'Pussy-whipped,' wasn't that what they called it back in high school? It was always 'my girlfriend this' or 'my woman that,' trying, in some way to say: I'm a man and I'm above that. But it was the fear of putting his own wishes forward that always brought her forth, as a mask, as a crutch.

As fall set in he'd noticed the futile tickets building up under the windshield wipers. And then they weren't there—and neither were the blades.

On a gray night as heat lightning flashed around the bowl of the heavens, he sat in the sash and watched the progress towards Devil's Night. Instead of soaping car windows some kids were taking the opportunity to have a bash at the hulk. The headlamps shattered with a light tinkling; the side vents took a lot more punishment. One of the sturdier lads wielded a fallen sign post like the top of the batting order, smashing home runs into the front and rear screens, while the rest of the team had some base hits into the windows. She'd come back late from classes and caught only the finale of the fête. He, unfortunately, was waiting for her curtain raiser, which consisted mainly of complaints about their state of affairs—which were less and less in the carnal sense—and the general despair she felt for their lives.

"It's not so much the blackouts where you start out fine and funny and end up screaming or crying or pissing on the mattress—on a *good* night—or the pushers dealing in front of us with lines of customers so thick you need a crossing guard to get through your own foyer and up the stairs. It's not even the fact that the heat and hot water are as consistent as the flip of a coin. Or the bugs and vermin. Or any of that. It's just that you don't even seem to care about it anymore. Not the services, not the drugs, not the crowds or the smell, or the noise or the humiliation by the scum of the earth . . . I don't even think you care about yourself anymore, let alone us." It was more than she'd said in the whole month. He suspected it had taken that long to finally reach a point of articulation. He wondered if the flash and thunder of the night had broken that barrier or whether it had taken someone else, like the batter downstairs, to open up this wind of disgust.

"I care . . . about you . . . when you're here. And that's rarely." There was something about the resignation in his voice taht reminded her of angostura, a dash of bitters at the back of the throat. "This new lateness of yours, the job and school, all get more attention than my needs. How can I be there for you when you're never here at all? Perhaps I'm a trifle selfish, but there it is. You're as frosty as this October... and I never thought summer would end."

At opposite ends of the room they held their corners, each slumped in the attitude of exhausted boxers. The silence between them now, blood on the canvas of the ring, cooling and drying into a permanent stain.

He broke it at last. "So what's it to be then?"

She spoke, the words dragged out like still-warm entrails. "I've talked with the girls and they agreed to let me stay with them. There's a spare room. It will do all right... for a time. Maybe a trial separation; it would give us time to straighten out our priorities."

With the last barriers to the world removed, the interior of the sedan took on the appearance of an overused dumpster. Green and yellow and tan and brown plastic bags began filling the cabin, almost as if it were some undifferentiated tissue now open to infection, to the cancer of the neighborhood. Even the trunk lid had been popped and now filled fast with all manner of garbage. He suspected it was leaking into the car's body from the condemned building, now half-crumbled before the wrecker's ball. The tableau of total decay mesmerized him. It appeared to degenerate and fester even while he slept or worked.

So it was something of a shock when he saw her bags piled up down at the curb and by the door. The man was stacking them into the van, the bay filling fast with her hodge-podge luggage, liquor store boxes, and trash bags with oddiments. He hid in the shadows of the construction awning, watching with amazement. She said something about Saturday being a good day for it as the doormen usually didn't come on until the evening. But he'd forgotten, or hadn't really believed it until then. As he considered the stunning parallel of the car's infection and the van's similar state, he was further staggered when she came out with a new load, the child-bride freshness of her beauty once more leaping into heart, and hugged the brawny loader as a lover.

He hadn't bothered coming back until after they'd gone. He knew that the feelings of betrayal would come out soon enough, along with the emptiness of the closet, the loneliness of the bed. But, first it was important to feel nothing, to kill all the sensations with as much numbing chemicals as possible: a few #5 yellows, a #10 blue, and Bacardi to keep it all down. Still, somehow, it wouldn't got away. It was much like the dead mouse he'd finally fereted out after several days, enduring an unknown stench that turned out to be the odor of decay. Probably one of the last civil exchanges between them was the acession from her that something did indeed smell 'funky' in the place. He was convinced that someone must be canning turnips in an industrial/commercial capacity downstairs. Finding the forgotten glue-trap and the corpse would confirm for him what he'd felt for days, how death was a thing that the body knew before the brain could figure it out.

As usual with late autumn, the season of trash fires was running concurrent with the Devil's Night craziness, both building towards that orgiastic climax of purging and cleansing before Halloween. Somehow, the public burnings and the private exhumation were merging in his mind but wouldn't quite settle into a coherent thought. Unwilling to let an oncoming revelation slip by, he sat down on the stoop, sipping the rum, as the first rush of the evening began piling up at the door. The desperate and indifferent were too polite to ask him to move; the doorman, however, was neither and not and did.

"Yo man, you can't sit here." The evil look in the mulatto was wasted in this case. "You got to move."

"Free." He said it as if to confirm something to himself, and then thought better of the communication. "Free country," he smiled back blithely. "Maybe you better call the police. I think they're supposed to handle the vagrants..." He turned to look towards the car, pointedly, to no one but himself, "...and the abandoned."

The doorman left him alone at that, unwilling to waste time and energy to deal with a user juicer. It was going to be a heavy business weekend.

From where he slouched now, he could see the graffiti standing out much clearer where it crossed the splattered enamel into the realms of rust. Squiggly lines and sharp geometries indicated some local hero's tag, the upturned martini glass logo of an avant-punk band, and some political slogans in Spanish. It had now become as much background scenery as the wall murals or the shop shutters and gates. The blinding vision finally struck him with the assimilation of these details, as bright as the fire just going up down the block.

'Was that it? The car is the tulpa, the energy-ghost of our love! It arrives as the harbinger of doom, then, as it becomes used by the street in every relationship possible from helper to haven to hopper...' Just as he was fogging through the mystery, CBS and Super J come out of the club and, with a few kind words on the side... "C'mon dude. We gonna get you off the street befo' y'get into trouble..." now help him into the storefront and set him up on a barstool by the door.

CBS holds up the half-empty pint and hands it back to him. "You know, dude, this ain't gonna kill whatever it is that's eating you up. This stuff turned my old man old fast. What is it? You unhappy 'cause youre old lady left you? Shit. That bitch done you no good, s'far as I can tell. 'Sides, it been gone for as long as that Charlie she lef' with been comin' roun'. You still with me dude?"

He saw staring out the door at the car, trying to complete the thought, the thought competing with the refrain: 'The husband is always the last to know.' "Yeah. I'm still here. I'm just a little left behind."

"Say what? Left behind? Shit! You a homeboy now." CBS slapped him on the back and smiled that charm. "It ain't no big thing. Jus' another change, y'dig it?"

"C'mon, Santana. It's your shot," Super J beckoned with a cue.

CBS called out, "Yeah! Lissen' you chill here for a while an' go on up an' sleep it off, okay? Got's to get back to my game." With that he went back to the pool table.

He moved the stool closer to the doorway so he could watch the whole street, thinking that, perhaps, the total view would bring back the answer that he was still seeking. 'Helper to haven to hopper. The world adapts to the intruder and the intruder changes to fit in. Is this the lesson here? Purpose imprisons us all...or does it? If form follows function does a change in form create a change in function? It certainly does here! Is this car/street relationship a true symbiosis? Or is it a host/parasite situation? Are any of us truly ever free?'

Even as he swivelled his head to gather more impressions the only salient points to garner were that the 'Brown Door' crew was getting together a squad. It took a casual, disinterested observer like him to see anything significant in one of their number detaching himself from the group and saunter across the street, towards the car. He looked quite harmless unless you concentrated on the wine bottle in his fist...and the wick in its neck. Before there was any stirring at all, any notice, the rag was lit and the molotov cocktail pitched into the rear window.

The car went up in a roar, the red-gold flame billowing out as coils and balls of smoke, energy clouds. The members of teh club pushed past him, knocking him to the pavement in their haste. He rolled over in time to see the construction awning catch fire, the flames crawling up it like roses on a trellis, bright thorns searching for a purchase in the old timber. He felt a wetness in his side and found the broken bottle wedged in his hip, the blood and the brown rum mixing freely.

At the first pop he turned from his wound to watch the low-caliber bullets register hits on CBS, his body jerking, rippling almost, with each impact. Three, four, five, and six, as he crumpled folding onto the sidewalk, a balloon man deflating. Within seconds they were alone, the sirens, the crackle of burning wood, the last gasps of CBS, these were the things that stood out of the night.

He now realized that they were all free, as free as turnips in a trap, as a dirving spirit loosed from the confines of metal to return to pure motion, as a seller of dreams given the long sleep, as he was, there, the blood and rum flowing together in rivulets down the concrete, free as his vital fluids, as his love was free, and only the pain remained...like the scent of death...and that was fading, leaving as fast as the fire advanced.

Hegira to Avenue C

BY DONALD LEV

TO THE EAST 10TH STREET BLOCK ASSOCIATION, the old Albert Hotel was a threat, a scourge, a blight on the community. To me, it was home sweet home. I'd lived there for a year and a half in a room on the second floor with a big picture window from which the gorgeous panoramic view of the word DAITCH was clearly visible in any weather, stretched across the top of the grocery across the street. The Albert was so convenient. I happened to work at the *Village Voice* at the time, diagonally across the street, and did most of my drinking right next door in the Cedar Tavern. So my life was very contained and convenient…thirty bucks a week for the room, which even boasted a carpet and a sink. If I hadn't met that waitress with the hallucinations and the chronic restlessness, I would never have left to make my hegira to Avenue C.

Alice and I met in the Cedar one foggy night in the spring of 1971, she complaining that her feet hurt and she was paying too much rent. We very soon agreed to throw our meager fortunes together by sharing a double room at the Albert. The first thing Alice did after we moved in together was to lose her job. The second, third, and fourth things she did was complain. First, the room was too small. We took a bigger room. Next, the elevator never worked. Then she started in on the neighborhood. "Marshall, you know it's boring, stuffy and stuck-up. No one ever talks to you."

"So if this is such a bad neighborhood, what do you call a good neighborhood?"

"The East Village. I used to live on Avenue A. I used to drink in Stanley's and the Annex and listen to jazz at Slug's and the Old Reliable. It was such fun."

"You actually *lived* in the Lower East Side?" I asked with a new respect. It was for me always an area covered with mystery romance and danger in which I had never been able to live. I used to read my poems sometimes at Rissa Korsun's open readings in Trinity Lutheran Church on 9th and B, and in 1967 or '68 I had a great reading in a coffee house on 10th Street that became the Diggers' Free Store. I read my most popular poem of the time and women showered me with their phone numbers—"Call me soon, I'm leaving for Paris in four days!" (I've never been lionized before or since.) I also remember the early '60s, the big pad on East 5th Street where Dylan stayed along with dozens of other subsequently famed folk music stars. It was divided up into cubicles like a Mexican whore house...but instead of whores there were some of the potentially biggest names in show business. Then there were the sullen mysteries of Tompkins Square Park where once a guy turned on me with knife and I opened an umbrella and he went away...and the Peace Eye Book Store...and St. Marks Place and the B&H and Ratner's!

"You actually lived there?"

"For two years, till I had a fight with my roommate and moved to Bleecker Street."

"You know I always dreamed of living in a storefront on the Lower East Side and throwing some books in the window for sale and having poetry readings every night, maybe get one of those coffee urns and have some coffee...people could bring wine or beer..."

"Oh, Marshie, how marvelous! Let's!" she chimed in the little-girl voice she put on whenever she wanted to be sure to influence me.

So the next day I took me down to Turk's Realty where many an East Village pad was to be had, and came up with a genuine storefront on East 9th Street and Avenue C. (The spot is presently a vacant lot in which some attempt has been made to garden.) The rent was $125 a month, which believe it or not for that time and in that location was on the high side.

Also the condition of the place probably made any rent at all on the high side. The landlord had said he didn't want any exposed brick, to leave his plaster on. Well, I thought, there was no accounting for human taste (at that time, exposed brick was the *sine qua non* of Bohemian trendiness). I happened to spot a bit of the wall where the plaster had already been pulled off and was feeling the brick and realized the brick would come out like a loose baby tooth if I wanted to pull it out. The building was literally rotting away. It had a genuine tin ceiling though. And it was filthy! There was a little closet with a toilet in the back that had some spots of dried shit on the floor which I was never able to get up. And a bathtub which doubled as a table by throwing a loose door over it. You pulled the door off when you wanted to take a bath, brush your teeth or wash dishes.

To her credit, the first words Alice said when she saw the place were "Do you expect me to live here??"

Not to her credit was the fact that she instantly changed her mind and began pleading with me to seal the bargain immediately.

"Oh, please, Marshie! I don't want to stay in that horrible hotel with the horrible elevator and the people that never smile."

And so we gave Turk a month's rent and a month's security yet!

We didn't want to pay two rents, so we moved from the Albert within the week, carrying our stuff in suitcases and cartons across town by foot, and for the rest buying a mattress at the Salvation Army store on 1st Avenue and picking up some other odds and ends on the street and in some of the numerous "antique" shops in the area.

Mr. Miller, the manager of the Albert, said to me as we were on the way out, "You're making a big mistake, Mr. Cohen. You'll be back." Which surprised me. I didn't think he took so much interest in his tenants.

We moved early on a Saturday morning, which was to give us the better part of the weekend to clean up the place. I cleared out a section for a kind of bedroom, for which I roped and curtained off about a third of the store with beads and drapes and cleaned that space for the mattress and the bedding and figured we'd really start cleaning up. "Marshie," said Alice in her baby voice. "Would you mind if I took a little nap?"

"Well, OK. I'll start cleaning up. But I can't do it alone. You know we don't have maid service here and I'm a bit out of my element."

"I'm sure you'll think of something," she responded in a voice that was almost threatening.

I realize, dear reader, I am not going to have your entire sympathy when I complain to you that every lick of work done in that store, I did. Alice lay there sleeping or sat up imperiously drinking. But she never lifted a hand to anything! What did I expect? What do you mean, what did I expect? We'd only known each other a few weeks. If only I had known about her extreme fatalism, I might have been forewarned.

"Back in North Dakota, you were supposed to marry as soon as you got out of high school. I thought if you wanted a boy to marry you, you didn't go to bed with him. There was this boy I liked, and didn't go to bed with him. So he married the first girl who did. Then I went with another boy who went in the Army, so I decided to join the Marines. When I got to South Carolina for boot camp, it turned out I was pregnant. I tried so hard to get rid of that baby but it still came. So they kicked me out of the Marines. Then some people were going to Florida so I gave the baby away and went with them. I worked at Junior's. Then some people were going to New York, so I came here. That was fourteen years ago."

Whatever the area in which we now lived might have been in the '60s, by 1971 it was a completely Spanish-speaking country, except for a dozen or so assorted gringos who mostly hung out in one old rundown bar on Avenue C, the only joint around where English was spoken at all. I was beginning to improve my high truancy high school Spanish trying to deal with the corner bodega. The local mothers decided the only reason Alice and I could be in that storefront was that we must be running a day care center, so while we were trying to clear out space to set out our supply of used books, the mothers would bring in their children and insist the kids stay with us while they went to the store. The kids were cute, wildly energetic little nuisances, knocking over books and shelves the second they were set up; so, after the novelty wore off, we found it impossible to cope with the phenomenon. Especially Alice who, try as she did to be kind, really hated kids. So we tried to discourage the day care notion as much as possible. One thing that made it hard was there wasn't much for those kids anywhere...the street was rotting and burning away. No day would go by without at least one appearance of fire engines on our block. A kid once said, "See we burn there, tomorrow we burn the school." Another kid said, "I like to be in the street, but I don't like going home at night." I could imagine, projecting from the condition of our store, what those tiny steaming rotting-away apartments must have been like, overcrowded with sparsely employed adults and confused unhappy children.

However "we," meaning mainly "I," set to work to make our place more like a bookstore (we named it the Old Planet Book Shop after a line in a poem I once wrote) presenting for sale mostly Alice's and my own collections of books—mine were literary and historical, hers, occult. Later on we bought some books from the three-for-a-quarter stalls of stores more advantageously located to the west, and marked them up to a quarter apiece for resale in the remoter East. Also some of the neighbors brought us books. The best sellers were usually the green covered reprints of Olympia Press erotic masterpieces, which we got rid of for half a buck apiece. We set up an electric coffee urn we had bought from the Salvation Army with a gallon of half Maxwell House, half Bustelo which was offered to the public free or for voluntary contributions.

And we'd have poetry readings every night but Thursday (which was Rissa Korsun's night at Trinity Lutheran Church). Friends would come by to read: Rissa, Fritz Hamilton, Dick Whipple (when he wasn't agitating on behalf of Mental Patients Lib), Barbara Holland and John Payne. By this time Alice was writing a little too. Such epics as:

"The girl in the red dress grew horns.
From that day everyone left her alone.
Everyone but the Devil, that is..."

We had one reading that packed them in. That was Ed Bullens and a very good looking, very fine poet named China Clark. The store was packed like a can of sardines with mostly white folks, and Bullens (who was a nice mild-mannered guy when he wasn't reading poetry) was letting us have it with both barrels with his machine-gun verses. One member of the audience, a poet named Rice Burns, who was something of a Southern gentleman, looked like he was very anxious to escape and I'm sure he would have run out if he hadn't been hemmed in by the rest of the crowd.

Of course, the readings tended more toward the other end of the spectrum, as when Serge Gavronsky, a very professorial translator of French classics, came downtown from Columbia to read his own poetry and nobody came. There was just Serge, me, and Alice, and the urn of coffee. But we had a nice visit anyway, drinking coffee and reading poems.

Outside of the poets we knew who dragged themselves out to the Far East out of friendship, and a few others who lived in the area, very few New Yorkers ever came to the store. I can only guess they were afraid of the neighborhood. But people came by from just about everywhere else. A couple of German poets dropped in, a girl from Poland, tourists from California and New Jersey... and other people who were on more exotic trips would come in to display their stigmata. I was thinking of converting the store into a religious article emporium if I couldn't relocate further west.

One particular lad accosted Alice and me on East 10th Street as we were trying to haul a book case we had bought from a used furniture store back to Avenue C. As we were struggling with our burden, a shirtless and shoeless young giant emerged suddenly from Tompkins Square Park, and declared he had just walked down from Boston to find us. He wanted to share some writings with us and therefore would help us with the bookcase, which he summarily lifted over his shoulder. Bowed under it, looking very much like Jesus carrying his cross, he proceeded on toward the store.

William (he said his name was) was a very nice young man around 20, whose writings were wild, prophetic and inscrutable. He came around a few times and we fed him and read each other's poems. Then he disappeared.

Another mystic among our regular "customers" was an older, rather stocky black man named Joseph who either was, or was in contact with, the main "hidden master" of the Theosophists. I guess he was drawn mainly by Alice's books, which he talked about but never bought. One uncanny night, we were sitting around drinking coffee, when all of a sudden, he said, "Shh. In a few minutes a visitor from Egypt gonna walk through that door." Nothing happened and the conversation went elsewhere for a while, then, about a half hour later, through the open door of the store walked this black cat, who looked at Joseph, then over at Alice, licked his whiskers once, then sat down and began cleaning himself. "There he is, fresh from Egypt, like I am," said Joseph. "That cat is a great mystic and he'll hang around here if he wants to and bring you luck."

The cat did seem to adopt us, and for several days stayed without that much encouragement from us beyond an occasional saucer of milk and piece of Puerto Rican white cheese and sausage (a staple of our diet). The cat would usually sleep with us, which for some reason seemed to make Alice nervous. More than once she said she wished that cat would go away and not come back. Then, after a week or so, the cat did go away and not come back.

Around this time, Alice started setting up a little shrine. She propped up a Bob Dylan album cover—it was "Highway 61 Revisited"—against the back of a wooden folding chair and set up a red candle she'd bought at the bodega on some piled-up bricks in front of the chair. Later she added a statue of San Miguel from a nearby *botanica* (which is a kind of Spanish occult store). I asked her once or twice what she thought she was up to, but got either no reply at all or one so evasive it might as well have been silence. I soon gave up trying to fathom the mystery. I knew we were playing a lot of Dylan records over and over on my old Webcor phonograph, and the music was getting us through claustrophobia and depression. I remember also the biggest hit song on the radio was John Denver singing "Country Roads" and that song seemed to me also very anti-depressant and anti-claustrophobic. We should have had a shrine to John Denver as well, but we didn't.

Another frequent habitué of the store was a septo- or octogenarian who went by the initials "J.J." J.J. wanted to give weekly lectures on sex in our store. Alice put her foot down on that one. "I don't want that dirty old man using my place for his games," she said. Another "steady customer" was a young fellow named Joe who wrote some pretty fair poetry but was prevented by dyslexia from putting much of it on paper. He'd come around and dictate poems and I'd type some of them for him. One of the most fascinating characters I have ever met was a neighbor who lived in the building next to our shop but one. His name was Chuck. A young black man in his mid- to late twenties, he held down some sort of steady job as a rent-a-cop. But his main claim to fame was that just about every night he left his sleeping body and flew. That's right. Flew. Astral projection, it is called in some of Alice's books. Not only that, Chuck claimed he would do things like break up fights, and prevent thefts and muggings, and be like a veritable super-hero at night, till his master, Papo, explained that doing stuff like that, no matter how worthy it seemed, constituted interference with other people's karmas. "In other words, if you were going to get mugged, say, it was probably something in your past life you were paying for, and my preventing that left you still owing and delayed your progress to a higher state. Dig?"

Chuck was a regular at a little spiritualist church on C near Houston, led by Papo. The rest of the congregation was entirely Spanish-speaking, but Papo was a powerful mystic and medium and could communicate on any level he wanted. He was also a great healer. Chuck invited Alice and me to come with him some night to the church. Papo and the other mediums ("there were many great mediums in the congregation") would be able to tell if we had any kind of trouble and would be able to heal us. I told Chuck we'd think it over, but Alice piped up, "Maybe you could get them to exorcise that awful noise you make all the time." She was referring, rather gracelessly, to a kind of verbal tic I had, and still occasionally have, which is hard to describe but I represented it in a poem once with a lot of h's . . . hhhhhhhhhhhhhhhhhhhhhh . . . like that.

"Well, why not give it a try?" I agreed, with feigned sanguinity. At least we'd get out of the store for a while. So we agreed on the following Tuesday night (we had to cancel a reading, but what the hell . . .).

So that Tuesday, we closed the store up around five and went to Chuck's apartment (he seemed to have a lot of the same books as Alice) and he offered us some wheatgerm and seaweed, but we demurred on account of we had already had our usual salami and white cheese sandwiches and quarts of Ballantine ale. Soon we embarked on foot down to Houston Street and the heart of darkness.

The church was the cleanest in a row of storefronts the east side of the cracked-up block between 1st Street and Houston. The shingled sign said "Iglesia Spiritualista San Miguel" and gathered about the entrance were many men and women with pleasant Latino and Indian-looking faces. Chuck introduced us to Papo. He was a tall, heavyset, square-jawed man dressed in a comfortable-looking brown suit with his collar tied with a leather string tie. Chuck had told us what a terrific "aura" Papo had, and you know, I could see it. I'm not a big believer in the occult, but certain people do have stronger "presences" than others, like actors when they're on stage, or successful politicians or businessmen. Papo and I just said "hello" and I felt this kind of electric current buzzing from his brain to mine.

The service was kind of simple and shamanistic. Papo and about a dozen other mediums, both male and female, stood in back of the storefront, facing the congregation who were sitting on chairs and benches. There were about sixty people counting both mediums and congregation. Everyone started singing hymns in Spanish. The hymn-singing went on for quite a long time and seemed to take on a kind of chanting rhythm and Papo and the mediums were kind of swaying a bit, just like you might if you were getting into the music . . . I think from what Chuck said beforehand that they were going into a trance. Then the singing faded away, and one at a time the people in the congregation would stand up and one or sometimes more than one of the mediums would speak to them in Spanish. By and by, after it seemed that everyone else who wanted advice or healing had been attended to, Chuck whispered to Alice to stand. After a moment, Papo began addressing her in English. "You have a very bright orange aura. A quick sharp spirit guides you. You can be a great medium."

Then it was my turn. Papo said, "I see a spirit beside you causing you grief. It is a foreign spirit, maybe French. If you come back next week we'll exorcise it for you and you will no longer have this problem."

Later, when we got home, I said to Alice, "Hey, I'm very impressed. They said you could be a great medium. What do you think?"

"Bullshit."

"Really? I thought you were into this kind of stuff."

"First of all, they do this astral projection stuff. Brownie warned me about that. It's very dangerous and anyway isn't good for you."

"Who's Brownie?"

"He was my teacher. And he was a lot better than you ever were."

"Oh."

Anyway, she didn't want to go back to the church. I decided that since I had this French spirit on my shoulder, I should try to make friends with him. I christened him "Balzac" and dedicated a poem to him. So much for our first and last formal religious experience together.

But now things were beginning to happen to Alice that were very frightening. She always did have weird drunks, getting a shade psychotic and seeming to slip into other personalities, seeing and hearing things ... she had told me she'd dropped a lot of acid with her husband (who she said was a satanist) and she was never quite right since. Now in the store all these things became very pronounced. She'd spend less time active and more time either sleeping or drinking. And the personality changes became more blatant, a la *Three Faces of Eve*. One of her personalities sounded like a very tedious Britisher. Another was a German boor who was extremely anti-Semitic and unpleasant. I nicknamed him "the General." One day she kept slipping in and out of this particular persona, who was ordering me around like a Nazi SS chief. The next morning, when Alice was pretty much entirely Alice, I told her that I could put up with a lot, but if that fucking general ever came back it would be the last time ... It never came back.

Meanwhile, I got fired from my job at the *Voice*. Now anyone who has ever had a little independent bookstore of any kind knows it takes years of being supported before it ever comes near supporting you. And the last thing I needed was to lose my job. What happened was, there was a riot one night in our neighborhood, in fact, all over the Lower East Side. We had only been there a few weeks. Long files of local citizens were doing a conga up Avenue C breaking store windows and looting stuff. I decided it would be wiser to hang out on the street with The People than to be huddled behind locked doors with the Bourgeoisie. Since I had worked this job on the *Voice* for a couple of years without taking one day off, when I called in the next morning to say I wasn't coming to work, instead of just calling in sick, I told my boss, a very flamboyant lady, the truth. "Antoinette, you'll never guess what happened. They had this riot all over my neighborhood, and I figured I'd better hang out on the street all night to protect my store. So I gotta get some sleep now. I'll be in bright and early tomorrow."

"The hell you will. You're fired."

"Fired? Why??"

"You know very well. The one thing I won't tolerate. Conflict of interest."

So with Alice getting sicker and crazier every day, and with no steady income, and the book business not exactly booming, and the neighborhood up in arms, it seemed time to end the hegira. I don't know exactly what we expected from the Lower East Side. I don't know exactly what Alice and I expected from each other. So I'm not sure what we brought out of the experience except a continuing sense of mystery. Or, rather, a sense of continuing mystery.

So we returned to the Albert to be welcomed by Mr. Miller himself. "Welcome home, Mr. Cohen. I told you you'd be back." And, mysteriously enough, he was patient about our rent payments for quite a while.

In the Garden of East

BY ZOE ANGLESEY

I touched the frame of his doorway
leading to a peristyle
visited by his dream the week before

Trailways sped me to the table
where he sat sparring gumbo style.

I had to stop.
Saw Erzuli prompting him
to take on Jesus.

He waved a walking stick impatiently
to clear the sky of lead and confetti.

Recruiting newcomers to the East River
for phase one screening
he threw down wads of bubblegum
then upped the wattage of the highnoon sun.

Laughter seemed more vital than breath.
Besides he introduced himself
as the fireater from the Lower East Side.

He rode a rickety bike
right on by allnight bodegas.

His teeth of coconut meat
wet with its rum laced milk
I tongued until the night gave out.

Notebook:
Sept. 13, 1983-April 4, 1984

BY ALLEN GINSBERG

5 AM OCTOBER 4, 1983—WOKE AT 4:30 AM, SLIGHT headache, having smoked cigarettes, after several days health.

Waking mornings in clear Fall sunlight with Flatiron shadowless green and stark shining under blue sky; cliffs.

I'd dreamt we were in a car, with Gregory Corso maybe—but not having writ the dream an hour ago when I woke, 'tis vanished.

A mild chill thru the dark window screen, the roar of a silent night's few cars passing in the roads below Bluff Street—a few lights shine, blue vapor lamps, in the arcades of the university.

Mornings I've been exercising this week half a dozen pushups, a dozen knee bends, standing a minute on my head, rolling backward on my spine, bending left & right, touching my toes—then Tai Chi, elegant. All my life I resisted morning exercises, now my beard whiskers grey & belly paunchy, and blood pressured backachey, I begin to limber up and guard "The Temple of the Body."

Visiting acupuncturist Jym MacRichie, who suggested a "change of lifestyle" of overwork anxiety and morning depression, I began in last half year to alter teaching and publishing lives—quit Naropa, get an agent Andy Wylie to manage my book affairs, do some exercise, move back to N.Y. to unify my life with my files office telephone paperwork long postponed collected poems to be surveyed, essays, interviews, etc. A longing to go home and be myself.

Yet in summer when I visited my apartment in the city, the heat smog humidity stench and sulfur color of sky and street dust gave me to think I was living in Hell City—the inhabitants violently inclined to each other on my street—

At the corner of 12th St and 1st Ave where the telephone booth often was smashed, glass sides shattered, where I took taxis uptown or to East Side Terminal for planes to Florida & Oregon—a house front window the Mafia's shewing dolls for sale before the green curtains that hide the card tables and counters inside the door.

Further down the street, when I walk home, 419's doorfront, day and night a couple guys hang out guarding the hall painted blood red where Heroin's sold.

Garbage lining the curb, or piled across from the Heroin doorway at the boarded up doorgates of an abandoned bus terminal or auto storage one storied building belonging to the church downstreet, from which garage building roof several years ago I was shot in the upper arm flesh by BB gun. Now the long abandoned building's sidewalk's often piled with refrigerators thrown away, sofas with holes burnt & stuffing blackened showing, broken chairs & boards, cans, bottles, watery piss and cockroachy-blackened metal enameled kitchen cabinets bent & decayed.

Along the other side of the street, a school with courtyard where kids sit gossip scream fight murder shoot up smoke & lounge at 4 AM, and a church front directly before my window'd apartment on 4th floor opposite the copper frieze above the doorway arches.

And a funeral home at the corner, with backdoor next to the church-alley entrance where Bingo's played by the ladies, in the alley garbage cans neat and plastic bags piled for the machine truck pickup every other day now, seems.

Below my window, my side of the street, the iron framed doorway of the cigarette smuggling storehouse—cars and small trucks from New Jersey limousines with big trunks mostly, come & deliver cheaper cartons from New Jersey, less tax, so smuggling from across the river for sale in Lower East Side neighborhoods—And at the curb a car every day—new ones, being repainted & refitted with license plates or sprayed a new finish or engine restored—the stolen car ring's curbside garage.

And at 6 AM the iron-like bells of the church clang electronic thru sounddishes on the roof between bell towers. Sunday mornings a crowd dress't in white and fresh lace and Sunday pants and hats goes up & down the church's front steps into the big wooden doors.

Returning from Berenice Abbott's Maine house lakeside, I thought of photographing the street, my own long lived in East 12th Street's unique broken steps, fence rails, vans painted purple with flash-winged adornments, spray-paint signs and basement steps, boarded up windows and Heroin guardians at the hallway door half way down the block.

20 January 1984 3 AM

Descending IRT stairway from 125th St elevated platform to street with young friend Steven the musician, a cop young cop with black visor cap & blue uniform patrols behind us—I think he's after us, listening in—"The chair" I hear in the distance around the corner on the street below—

The young policeman rushes forward—it wasn't us after all as thought—he's bounding forward so swiftly I don't see him turn the corner—a scuffle, shouts, we come to the street & look down past the cars & 5 floor apartment buildings, a group of policemen in confusing struggle with seems two arabs, dressed as sheiks—Jamaicans or Mohammedans?—

The larger arab in burnoose & flowing robe shakes off the young cop & 5 others trying to lay hands on him—The other raises himself up back to the buildingside walls & pushes all the cops away—They square off down street—How can these arab thugs get away with that, resisting arrest—for stealing chairs?—No couldn't be that—But the police are scared—They don't want confrontation not with those rifles—long guns the sheiks have—waving them in air, if the cops want to start something they better watch out, and they are! It's a stalemate, authority's reversed, like the moment I challenged the two muggers in my apartment hall door downstairs, and suddenly realize I should have ignored them & fled upstairs & got help rather than dubiously taking them on at that spot where they had me alone—

So they took either side of me, one pulled a knife—shorter of the two, pale hispanic cheeks & thin moustache—& they went thru my pockets, felt my sox, into my breast pocket, thru my wallet for $8.00, my Helsinki fur hat, my halting watch—and slipped out "Come on Chico"—I was surprised, calm, later a little stunned—what to do? Upstairs called the police, who arrived in a car & toured the neighborhood with me in the back seat looking for "two hispanics" one long & other short & thin with porkpie hat.

These arabs in dream reversed power roles with police.

When I woke, the high grunt of power truck, the garbage behemoth was parked in the snow under the yellow sodium vapor streetlamp in front of the schoolhouse across the street, groaning metal & moaning iron gears, trying to eat up snow? No its iron lip had a black plastic garbage bag edge half chewed in its rear tooth gate—They chugged & moaned at the curb, then the two attendants settled in the front cab lit cigarettes & suddenly drove off after 15 minutes roaring at the curb trying to digest the Catholic garbage.

7:25 AM

"You have to hand your parents the plum"

We're rehearsing in a cabin in Maine-California by the sea inland. The song is Joni Mitchell's. I've never understood her chord changes and tuning.

She bends over the lead sheet and sings it, line for line. Steven Taylor and I bend over the music and try to follow. He understands the notes and the chords in relation to the words, I don't. I'm worried at my own incompetence. How will I edit my own collected poems, if I don't understand these basics that others do understand?

"Aw it's too hard" I think—I want to lift my head and go away. Steven stops me: "You have to make it perfect in this lifetime, it's your only honorable chance to complete your work, to make it completely clear, to encourage your genius, you have to do it, that way you can be proud of yourself" continues 24-year-old English-born Steven, "You have to hand your parents the plum."

I awake, a giant truck parked by the church across the street is breathing in the snowy January street as a few birds far up in blue morning sky pass puffs of grey chimney smoke and higher beyond the church tower's copper dome dusted with snow a tiny plane floats passing by to Kennedy or La Guardia airport—The radio's silent the radiator knocks steam rising behind the 6 room apartment's south window in the living room where I have a long desk board set up on two olive-grey file cabinet supports.

"How many more years do I have to inhabit the divine sepulchre" I thought writing last nite's dream.

1/29/84 N.Y.C.

Up late Sunday, late nite reading thru N Y Times
Danced slow motion Tai Chi once,
boiled water, hot lemonade purifies the liver
Twice more the 13 steps of Tai Chi,
cleaned my face, teeth, altar in my bedroom,
filled seven brass cups with water & laid them out straight rowed
Sat for an hour—Why'd the N.Y. Times call Living Theatre riffraff
Has CIA taken over culture? am I a mad bohemian with bad bile?
The steamheat radiator burned down ancient forests,
my window was open, excess heat escaped
I could hear chattering & cries of children
from the church steps across the street—

well dressed adults stepped out fur collared.
as I looked up from my pillow—
hundreds of fluffy snowflakes filled the air
above East 12th Street's lamps & cars
floating down like dandelion seeds from grey sky
floating up and drifting west and east by the fire escape.

1/13/84—

Snow on the red painted iron fire escape, slush on the steps of the church across the street, "Mary help of Christians," looking out into the grey sky above the roof corners south there's a little Greek Orthodox cross on the roof corner of the church on 9th St. at Tompkins Square Park, and a little squared-off cross in the sky sitting on the granite winged globe that tops the Mary church roof. And the redbrick slum school's got its own elegance elevated in the winter-clouded heaven-palladian white-stone scrollwork & cones set up on roof-facade arches, actually elegant, I never noticed before trying to write the following dream, up awake at 8:30 AM Saturday morning, sat at my father's desk in my own bedroom on East 12th Street same week Peter's sanding the apartment floor next door to move in with his girlfriend Juanita.

Several days ago I dreamt of a child murderer, a young boy in earlier than adolescent years who was caught by an older man for committing mass murders or some similar woe.

I just woke from a dream whereat I was at a Moonie-like convention in a permanent city park, many families and children there with their cars and dogs, many State Department respectables and government thieves and servants—all very middle class good Americans. It was a patriotic park, like Disneyland, a right-wing political park, in fact Henry Kissinger was attending the park this weekend as well as myself and friends perhaps Peter & Louis Cartwright Huncke's friend, and a mass of civilian and army wives and infants and uncles—what was I doing there?

The ceremonies were public but there were secret rites and certain areas wherein only the initiated could enter with their children—a little fearful, the commitment, and as I was present I wondered if I'd influence anyone in future generations or present to accept this gruesome political cult as kosher acceptable. I was just there as an American seeing what was going on in popular culture—and I'd run into the neighbor's kids and we'd walked together along the grassy paths in a sheep meadow (like in Central Park). Still there was this mysterious and secret grassy bank and hidden mountain-cave area, entrance wherein put you under the power of a strange inhuman political death spell.

Isn't that like America, I thought awake, with Henry Kissinger presiding or attending the rites of a mass political religious death cult—a religion so widespread as to be unnoticeable, attended by the entire nation, with death cult and executions carried out in Central America and assassinations in U.S.A. and some hint of organized crime chiefs somewhere in the governing board, and some Kissinger keeper of many secrets as ambassador or counsellor on public relations to the death squad priests. An anti-communist religion, with life and death vows & rituals, and huge propaganda apparatus like the Vatican.

Snow shovels & bus noises in the street and the radiator's whistling steam heat while my brother's son Peter walks in the hall getting ready to move furniture and sand the apartment floor.

In Tom Clark's biography of Kerouac...K. reminds himself & vows to write something every day of his life. I'll do that now, age 57, after years of irregular attention to the word record of my portion of eternity.

1/17/84—4:10 AM Monday

Sat yesterday an hour—chanted evening prayers with Peter. Juanita sitting at kitchen table "you're always asking Allen his opinion." Wants to break him of that habit of intimacy with me. Well why not—open up space! Adventure alone in the East 12 Street apartment.

Will they shoot me?
Will they?
Am I not exempt?
Will I be an exile
In a desert tent?

A famous writer in a flat
In Rio on a hill?
Pursued by armies in the states
Hiding from His will.

The Editor of this book
is older now
Than poems that he wrote,
Stars on his brow.

Not to display
Were modesty
Greater than Nature
Tempted today.

Looks like I'll masturbate as main erotic completion till my deathbed. All my life looked for mortal lovers and had many but none at liberty for lifetime. Had always thought by 40, by 50, by sixty, issue settled bodily I'd find a love mate. By now the pattern seems clear to see there will be no "final" erotic solution or engagement with another I'll continuously desire & be able to get. Realized that last night settling on my side in the dark right cheek on pillow. What an obvious surprise—I should have realized that long ago and not hung on to phantasy so indefinite—how could it be different in future from past perform-ance? Is it that my ideal or phantasy has always been incompleteable, a young boy always will grow older—I'd have to find a pale muscled youth willing to embrace an older grizzled genius body self—Possible but not likely, and al-ready happened temporarily many times—Peter, Neal, L., Jimmy G., the Japa-nese and Venezuelan boys of mid sixties, Gary G. late sixties, Steven B. mid sixties on for five years, Jno. R., Steven T. mid seventies, David M. awhile at Naropa, Steven H., a few months, Bobby M. awhile, Richard W. awhile, George B. several years late '70s, Chuck C. in Boulder & Boston 19 years old & we hit it off for several years, then Brian J. still somewhat faithful—Certainly these 17 loves were gracious warm delight and all are still fond of me and I of them—If I had to go back, likely two, Steven T. & Brian still seem the most direct dear & desirable tho only Brian is still committed to lifelong love—but he's so young how can that last into my 60's? Amazing grace! More to come! Till I go! And another hundred loves from Milwaukee to San Francisco—Mark O! Jon S! Brad G! Gordon B! Chance loves in Worcester, Cambridge, kids from Lower East Side, Washington D.C., Spencer S. dead all others still alive! How lucky! Neal dead, Jack dead, only a few bodies vanished from Earth, the rest breathing memorable.

Thanksgiving 2 AM

From a Novel in Progress

BY RICHARD MEYERS

T WAS 1980. THE SUN CAME UP. MY EYES OPENED. UH OH. I've woken up again. The bed didn't smell good, but it smelled like home. It was the way the bedclothes seemed to crumble against my skin that was irritating. And then there was the morning light: strictly on schedule, empty and smug like a prison guard and so fucking ugly. It was infuriating, and that made me tired all over again. But here I was, waking up. I know what the problem is: I've gotten so skinny there's no distance between my nerve-ends and my brain and everything has too much impact... All that flooding light out there that people seemed to flourish in. The morning was like a big ocean pressing its moronic face against the windows and walls of my lost apartment, and there I was alone. I was sunk.

Still I was handsome and young.

I smelled my armpits. Oh no. I knew it anyway, I'd known it all along, but there it was, that smell. It had come up like a fragment of a dream suddenly recalled, just a little haunted feeling, like the snap of realization that what's different in the house is that something's burning. It wasn't the normal smell of sweat. It was the sharp chemical-metallic smell sweat glands make when they're deprived of heroin.

I'd made the mistake of waking up again. Terrible to start the day with a mistake. I was starting every day a little *behind* and it was mounting up until pretty soon I'd be dead without really ever having been born.

I threw the covers off. I couldn't stop thinking. It was spring. It had a smell to it too, even in New York. It smelled like just-cooked heroin. It was the exhaust fumes mixed with the wet air that still carried subtle hinted promises of voyage and growth. Sea air and foliage. The hot spoon of clear brown liquid had replaced all that. I thought of the crowds out there swarming over the streets with their minds clicking and buzzing and yawning with schedules and breakfast table slights and anticipations of the boss's reactions and big hopes and my mind went blank the way it does when a mathematical problem gets too complicated. I didn't get it.

I was alone and I thought, that's one good thing about heroin it keeps you conscious that you're alone. Still, I didn't want to die before I was born. My faith in myself was going. It had actually started years before but everything happens in slow motion with dope. You fall behind. It had just recently gotten serious enough that I had to notice it. I needed something to believe in.

I got up naked and in the same motion lifted my thick biker's belt from the doorknob beside the bed and slipped along the wall into the living room to avoid being seen through the living room window. I pulled loose the loop of string that held a roll of tattered bamboo halfway up the window and the shade fell with a sharp clatter like a pang of guilt gone in a second. I hung the belt over the back of a chair and went into the kitchen where I filled a glass with water and grabbed a handful of toilet paper. Back in the living room I put the paper and glass on the chair. There was a small hidden drawer in the table beside the window opposite the couch. I opened it, reached in and pulled out a spoon and syringe. The spot where I sat on the couch was permanently dented by my weight and radiated a broken fringe of cigarette burns. The spoon, which was black with carbon on the underside, held a crusty piece of cotton in the middle of a brown stain. This was the residue of my last shot of the night before. I sucked up some water from the glass with the syringe and squirted it into the spoon. Using the tip of the needle I loosened the cotton and swirled it in the murky liquid to dissolve every last encrusted grain. Then I lit a cluster of five or six paper matches and held it under the spoon. Get it sterile, make sure it all dissolves. It bubbled, a wisp of steam arose. It clarified. Everything was focused there. I pulled the fluid into the syringe through the filtering cotton, pressed the syringe free of air bubbles, tightened the belt around my bicep and slid the needle into the main vein of my forearm. I pushed the plunger out with my thumbnail and a thread of blood appeared in the liquid. A hit. I pressed the plunger in. Fuck. Hardly feel a thing.

Still I'd usefully killed five minutes. Now what?

I liked my apartment. I thought of it as a cave. When I was a kid in Kentucky we used to go cave hunting. There are lots of caves in Kentucky. In the open fields and pastures around the suburb where I grew up you could spot their likely positions where the ground was sunken and trees were left to grow. We'd take candles and sandwiches and flashlights and go exploring. Get really muddy. Find tiny animal skulls and salamanders. We would make a fire and cook up plans to run away and hide in the caves, live there, and only appear to civilization as guerrilla marauders, like Jesse James, popping up like hallucinations in supermarkets and raiding unlocked kitchens to pocket some bread and baloney and batteries, running through backyards, caught only for a flash in peripheral vision, escaping back to our hidden caves.

There was nothing worse than getting stuck though. The main object of every new cave exploration was to find a cavern as big as a room. We never did. But you never knew what a tunnel might lead to. That was the excitement. You'd push yourself inch by inch, crawling, timeless inch-diving through rock on your belly, squirming and squeezing in the chilly darkness, sweat and cave-water dripping in your eyes, sharp stone scraping the back of your head, in hope that the passage would open up like a castle. And then you'd find that you'd pushed yourself in so far that you not only couldn't go further but you couldn't go back. You were wrapped in rock and trapped. Claustrophobic panic would rise like gigantic internal missiles and then either explode or fall down dead. Sometimes the muscle-rockets would blow you far enough backwards to get free. Sometimes you gave up and that was great for a minute or two, dreaming of rot and revenge with your face in the tiny rivulets. Lovelorn jewels inside your eyelids. Then the fear and desperation would kick in again.

Never thought of that. I reached for a notebook to note the similarities between past and present. Couldn't see making a song out of it, but someday these notes would pay off. If I kept track of what seemed interesting or revealing or beautiful long enough to find out what was worth writing down I'd be able to look at it and know who I am, or was. Then make some serious revisions. Maybe I could even make something beautiful. I knew I was all out of focus. There was the me who was still and acted truly and knew what mattered and there was the me all battered and impulsive and torn by the bombardment of cheap shiny foreign ideas and they overlapped and shared loops and capillaries and were shadows of each other that kept me ugly and baffled.

It was 1980, but it could just as well have been 1880 or 1780. 1780 would be good. I'd be some cadaverous, over-refined ("Oh my God it's Spring again, I can't abide the din of those atrocious budlets"), end-of-the-line aristocrat, locked away in his decaying manse, miles of Spanish moss from the nearest Devil Dog or Ding-a-Ling...and then the impertinent sun comes up. Ugh. Brush a cobweb from my elbow...the vulgar sun: oppressive, tasteless, indiscriminately pushing itself upon the landscape again, uninvited, intruding upon my dusty bedchamber. Another day. I'd made the mistake of waking up again. "Again" is the codeword, the password: everything is again. Again and again and again.

"Morning. I get out of bed. "Time to start pretending!' " Boy it would be great to be a cartoon.

I needed to piss. Just got off and I needed to piss. That was bad. Meant I'll be sick again inside of two hours. I only felt normal. I wasn't really straight. I hated feeling normal, it was nerve-wracking. The only thing feeling normal meant was that you'd be sick again soon. It meant you were a little afraid. Impatient. Jumpy and angry.

I put away the works. I went and took a piss and then went into the bedroom and pulled on a pair of jockey shorts and a skin-tight pair of black levis that had a couple of small brown-rimmed holes in the thighs where I'd hung them too long inside the oven to dry one night when I had to play a gig. I always like clean clothes for gigs. I buttoned on a tight striped shirt with frayed sleeves cut off real high and pulled on a nice thick pair of socks that smelled all right. Then I carried the phone from beside my bed back into the living room and put it down beside my spot on the couch. I sat there.

I sat there. There was my dick inside my pants, really warm and heavy and potent. Maybe I should jerk off. I felt obliged to take advantage of every opportunity for any kind of relief. It would fill up another few minutes with fun. I hadn't come in days—it was like taking a shit, you could only do it between highs. The dust is falling. The skeleton pulls out his dick. Whoa. The pleasure, like piercing shards, like pieces of triangles skimming, banging around in your body. Whoa. God it happens fast when you're straight. Floods of it. And it's practically a convulsion, a little epileptic fit. You almost see stars. But then it's gone and all that's happened is you're a little emptier, too alert and skinned bare to even drift in the sweetness for more than a minute. Satisfied by slightness, as if you'd eaten too much popcorn. I pulled my pants back up. I let the feeling wash through me for its allotted time.

The sun was really up now, all the window coverings in the house were off and I felt overlit. The day was making its demands. Who should I call? Was everybody burnt out? There's always ten dollars somewhere. There's always twenty dollars. Did I have any books worth selling? Should I pawn my guitar again? That was always an option. It felt a little chilly in here. The spring was the coldest season because the outside temperature hovered around the level where the slumlords were legally required to turn on the heat and they exploited it for all they were worth.

The phone range. All right. My charm was intact. This had to mean at least ten dollars. Anyone who'd call me at this hour must know what they're in for. They're begging to be fleeced.

It's Chrissa. Bull's eye. She had a job and she cared about keeping me as a friend.

"Chrissa, I was just thinking about you."

"You were? Uh oh."

Damn. Is this trouble? Am I going to have to sit still for a lecture?

"What were you calling about?"

"To remind you we were meeting Duke…"

"Oh shit. I totally forgot…"

"That's why I'm calling. You don't have anything to worry about. Duke thinks you're great. He has big plans for you."

"Yeah, but I don't feel very good today."

"What's wrong?"

"Well, you know, I don't feel too well and I don't have a dime. I'm outta books to sell. I don't wanna pawn my guitar again. I've got rehearsal later and now that Jay down the hall is on the road there's no one to borrow one from easy. I got all the advances from the club I can get, but I'm getting a big check from my lawyer next week. I can't see Duke feeling like this… Lemme have twenty Chrissa and I'll pay you as soon as I get that check."

I really felt like a clown, teetering. When I asked her for money, my fate—pathetic loser or lovable poor artist—balanced in the tone of her reply. I hated this, but I was inured to it. It was like a greeting. Hello, how are you, can you lend me ten bucks. But I didn't want to fall.

Fortunately, I knew, Chrissa was hoping to benefit from this meeting with Duke herself and besides she didn't like to see me embarrassed.

"Okay, okay, you can have twenty dollars to pay me back next week. But you better be good with Duke. This is important."

"I will. I'll be top form. But listen, actually, do you think you could make it 23 so I can get some peanuts and a soda?"

"Johnny—"

"Now come on Chrissa, what's three dollars? But it'll make a big difference to me…"

"Oh all right, but you have to come over here now because I'm going out."

"I'll be there right away."

I hung up, feeling great and slimy at the same time. But in a flash the million-sunned heat of my unfailingly brilliant luck had baked the slime to a thin thin crust, it fell away, and I was pretty shiny again. Another eight hours arranged for.

Dealing with humans was always a drag. They forced me to lie. They always had to be made to feel that either they were going to get something from me or that I cared about them before they would give me any money.

● ● ●

Chapter 2

Off to Chrissa's. I didn't like being outside. I kept feeling like there'd be a loud noise and I'd jump. I thought how I'd lived here so long nothing looked new and interesting any more. It was hard to find a route where I wouldn't be likely to run into someone I knew and realize that they were worried that I was crazy because of the way I was trying to force myself to look into their eyes in order to show that I wasn't crazy, and then I'd have to make an abrupt excuse that made me seem even crazier and move off fast.

I was a machine that was set to skim, power-walk, to that doorway, collect, and move on to the next. I felt pretty good. I did like to see Chrissa. Someday I was going to have to pay her back, do something really nice. Like, um, a champagne and caviar dinner. Or better yet a trip around the world (with me). I bet we could have a really sweet, very sexy night together. I loved her breasts. I loved her butt. I'd like to ski off it. Or would she laugh me off? Just thinking about it made me feel cute. I hated it when she made me feel cute.

She knew me too well. I'd had to apologize too often. I'd confessed too much. (And I'd made the wrong confessions.) She'd seen my resolve fail too many times. Why am I going on like this? Am I a broken man? I laughed and a passerby glanced at me and looked away instantly.

Springtime: not hot enough for the garbage to smell. These old people with their dogs are ridiculous. How could someone let himself get old and wander around with a fleabitten hound on this vicious battleground? Well they're just wallpaper to me. But this existence needs some new wallpaper.

Then again, nothing ever changes. I could just imagine myself a time traveller and it all became interesting again. Where was I? I walked down Tenth Street where proud Puerto Ricans (after all, they'd survived to be teenagers and were making money at a good clip) exchanged little ticket-sized envelopes of marijuana for five dollars. Out in the sun like that the money always looked like it had a silver patina you could smudge with a thumb. As if it were magic and if everybody would stop pretending the stuff would just disintegrate.

I'd had a little epiphany, a little insight into the timeless state of things once when I was walking on 14th Street, the budget bazaar for the area, the most grotesque gallery of souls to be seen this side of the presidential cabinet. I'd seen everyone in the dignity of their fate, their origin, their condition as each one a separate manifestation of the earth's possibilities. And of course human-kind itself was just one example of what it was possible for the world to say. The self-determining animal one. But now I'm thinking the race is nearing its death and it's going to realize, like the artist in the Borges story, that its effort to fathom the universe and fulfill itself, the patterns it has created in striving for knowledge, beauty, and harmony (civilization and world domination) all merely add up to a self-portrait, and in this case it would be a very ugly, brutal, destructive, selfish face. The more lines that are added to the face of the earth, the more detailed and clear the subject of the portrait becomes, as we near our finish, and soon the world will erase us and return to the drawing board. Maybe dinosaurs will get another chance. They did better than we have.

Chrissa lived on the top floor of a building on St. Mark's Place. It shocked me mildly to see how I could resent her for forcing me to climb seven flights of stairs to borrow $23 dollars from her.

I get up there and she's sitting in the middle of the floor thumbing through a single-drawer file cabinet. A glance at her does two things to me: it makes me glad to be alive, and makes me feel left behind and shut out of life altogether. Damn damn damn. I don't like this real life, where actual people with their own desires and intentions can look at me, expect things of me, interpret my behavior, classify me; I like my mental life where Chrissa and I are together forever the moment we locked eyes seven years ago.

How did I get to be old enough to say "seven years ago"? If I can get to be 30 I can get to be 40. That throws a new light on things. How will taking that into account change the way I act? I'd been thinking about this question.

"Hi Chrissa, whatcha doin'?"

"I'm looking for some pictures for a job I got." She was a photographer.

"Oh. You know, I was just thinking about something. I read somewhere recently that the Greeks thought of the past as being ahead of them and the future behind. You know, because the past is what you actually see, it's what your eyes are open to, whereas the future... it's wherever your back is turned. And anyway it's mostly made outta the past. Kind of comforting don't you think?"

Groan. I was playing the fool because she made me feel at a loss.

"Yes, I know you'd like to put your future behind you."

"Don't be mean now. Don't be cruel."

"There's your money over there. I know you're in a hurry."

Ow. Fuck. I might as well have been a delivery boy. I used to delight her. I used to excite her. Well she was mad at me because she knew I was acting and it offended her.

"You know, those Greeks... how did they get to be so philosophical? It must be because they made up the word. But gee it seems like they saw the big picture all the time. It must have been because of their gods. When all we have are movie stars. See, their gods were like people, while we've degenerated into treating people like gods. Can you imagine if Liza Minnelli or Al Green or Clint Eastwood could turn you into a duck? That would make you philosophical."

She started laughing. Wow that was good luck. I still had a little juice. I could get out of here on a good note. I loved to make her laugh. It made me love her all over again.

(Oh Chrissa, this is to you. I will dream aloud the secret adventure that flimsy clumsy reality [me] was not tough and fine enough to carry. But that nevertheless occurred and is occurring still as if the figure and ground were reversed and the universe were made of earth and the world a hollow globe of visions that have created us as I describe them, the way light created eyes. I love you. See you around.)

But this was just a stop on my dope run and to whatever degree she knew or understood that, it was enough to make her despise me a little (with regret). This flaw in the moment was like a secret vanity of mine she'd discovered, as if she'd caught me posing in the mirror kissing myself, and it only made me want to leave sooner.

"I'd be a duck for Al Green," she said, getting a dig in, "but our god of the moment is named Duke and for reasons of his own he has a special fondness for you, which for all our sakes I hope you appreciate. I don't know how many more chances you're going to get—I admit you always seem to be able to find another one—but I'm wrapped up in this too…."

She sure could get cold. She wasn't giving me an inch. Well it was only sensible.

I picked up the money. "See you." And then, "I'm going to come through, Chrissa. I know you're right. Whatever this plan Duke has, if you think it's so interesting, it must be worthwhile. I'll be there today and I'll be in good shape."

I made her stand up and hug me before I left.

Back to the street, where I was King. Lord of the garbage. I went to cop.

Copping was about as interesting as waiting for a subway train. (Though God knows I was enthusiastic about it.) Nothing good could happen—there was never a pleasant surprise—it was just a monotony that always had the potential of turning into something worse.

I went on automatic again, pacing the most efficient route at a steady high speed sufficient to discourage all but the stupidest or craziest from thinking they might be free to detain me. I was on important business. I knew how to walk mean, with an expression of intimidating determination that was by you before you'd recovered enough to jump it, friend or foe.

Once I'd copped the bags, the trip home was a breeze. I was set free, nothing could shake me except for the reflexive anxiety that would push my fingers into the watchpocket of my jeans every couple of blocks to make sure the bags couldn't get dislodged. I felt like school was out. There was nothing else in the world I needed.

I leaped up the stairs to my apartment and had my shirt off before I got to the living room. I assembled my paraphernalia with a speed, precision of movement, and conservation of energy the equal of the finest mystic craftsmen of old. A tea ceremony.

In a moment I was high. The silence and inching shadows in my room were very beautiful when resonant with heroin, all anxiety dissolved. My writhing ceased; I was competent, I was good, I was in tune.

I had my notebook beside me, a 16-ounce bottle of Coke, and a bag of peanuts.

I was a ticker-tape machine of poetry, an acrobat of spiritual language who would even feign slips for the hair-raising grace and hilarity of my recoveries for God alone. God being all the dead poets. All and everything. The watcher who grows and branches and forgave me while hoping for the best. Me dreaming the world in my image where it radiated from my empty room where I was alone and happy.

I picked up a magazine and by total "coincidence" (one sees what one is alert to) read "There is no I . . . there is only God. It is He who glistens on the ocean's surface amid the orange groves; the heady fragrance is also He, and so is the wind, the snake, the shark, the wine. Do not see yourself as yet another dream; go on dreaming yourself." A little over-Biblical, and the guy (definitely a guy) must be Mediterranean, plus he's a little short in the shark department, but that last line has a good twist. I set to dreaming.

I shook my head and the tiny acrobats fell like spangles, like the cool rain on another planet, down to the inside of my feet.

I had to pull myself together. It was almost time to meet Duke.

Sam's Party

BY COOKIE MUELLER

T WAS HIS PARTY AND HE'D DIE IF HE WANTED TO.
Sam was that kind of guy. He never let anyone down, especially himself.

This particular party was for his birthday, at the apartment he shared with his lovers, Alice and Tom. All his loyal friends were there, the famous, the infamous, the wash-outs, the successful rogues, and the types who only have fame after they die. They were the representatives of the New York alternative sub-culture, the people who went to sleep at dawn, and never held a nine-to-five job because they were too odd-looking, or sassy, or over-qualified.

Because Sam had an M.F.A. degree, he never had any money, but he always gave great parties—never pretentious ones, always wild ones. He wasn't short handed with the food or liquor.

It wasn't even midnight but the party was already jammed and jumping. Alice hadn't even gotten around to lighting the candles on her attempted Cordon Bleu birthday cake when I noticed Sam thanking a rock star for a very small birthday present, one of the many very small presents he'd received all night—yet another glassine bag of heroin, his drug of choice. He'd been using it off and on for the past few years.

He immediately went to the bathroom with Tom and locked the door.

At first no one missed the host. The party was too good. The stereo was blasting rare old hits and obscure unreleased new stuff; people were dancing, laughing, drinking. The layered smoke in the rooms was a gray veil. The place was wall-to-wall celebrities and future stars, who all knew each other and were still speaking.

I was dancing on the sofa when Alice approached me looking a little worried.

"Where's Sam?" she asked. "Have you seen him? I want to light the cake."

"I think I saw him going out for more beer," I lied. Alice didn't like Sam using heroin, especially if she didn't get some of it.

Alice went to the door. Shoeless in her fishnet stockings, she walked out into the misty November night where the party was spilling over into the street.

"Sam?" she screamed lamely into the abyss of the Lower East Side tunnel of tenements. "Sam!?"

"Didn't see him out here, Alice," the people sitting in Sam's blue Pontiac convertible said. There were people on the stairs and on the ledge too, but they had'nt seen him for a while either. Meanwhile I knew Sam was very busy in the john, and by this time there was a line at the locked door. Everyone was getting impatient with their bladders full.

It wasn't three minutes later when Tom slipped out of the bathroom, closing the door behind him and holding the doorknob, making sure no one got in. He looked nervous.

"Hey, Tom, you finished in there or what?" a drag-queen film star asked him. She was the first in line.

"Go out on the street and piss," he said just as nicely as he could, and the drag queen thought this was not a bad idea, so she headed for the street. So did a couple of others in line.

While Tom was standing there holding the doorknob, I noticed he looked ashen and awful, like the blood had just drained from his head. Frantically scanning the room, he saw me looking at him and called me over.

"What's wrong, Tom? What's going on?" I asked him after I fought my way through the crowd. Tom's hands and even his hairdo were trembling. He was sweating all over his party silks.

"Come in here," he wedged the door open so we could squeeze in over protests from the line.

"Hey, come on... man, I was here first, Cookie..."

"Lettus jes take a quick pee."

Inside the bathroom, Sam was lying on the floor in a fetal position. His skin was the color of a faded pair of blue jeans. A syringe and a bunch of crumpled empty glassine bags were on the floor, next to him.

"Obviously he's O.D.ing! Do you know what to do?" Tom was beside himself. He guessed I might know because for years I'd been writing a sort of "health in the face of drug use" column for a downtown newspaper.

"Yeah, don't worry, Tom. There's time before somebody dies shooting too much heroin. It never happens in a flash, despite what you've heard. DON'T PANIC! Just go to the kitchen and get some salt—and some ice cubes," I said. "And hurry."

While he was gone, I filled the bathtub with the coldest water possible and tried to lift Sam into it, clothes and all, but he was dead weight. He may as well have been a Buick. I had to wait for Tom but he was probably having a hard time making his way through the mob of plastered party people. Whe he finally returned, Alice was with him. She started to wail, then tried to kiss Sam awake, which never works.

"Let's get him into the tub," I said. So we lifted him in.

"This water's freezing," Alice cried.

"It's supposed to be," I told Alice.

"I DON'T HAVE TO PEE, I HAVE TO SHIT," someone outside the bathroom said, banging on the door.

"Do we have any time?" Tom asked.

"He's going to die . . . on his birthday . . . he's going to die!" Alice was weeping over the tub, her tears falling on Sam's blue face.

"He won't die," I said.

"WE KNOW YOU'RE DOING DRUGS IN THERE! WE DON'T WANT ANY, JUST LET US PISS!" The banging at the door kept up.

"Any ice cubes?" I asked Tom.

"None. I was fighting over the last ones in somebody's vodka." Tom was sweating again.

"DAMMIT, GUYS . . . WHAT THE HELL YA DOIN IN THERE? COUNTING TOILET-PAPER SHEETS?" Somebody in line was really mad.

"What's the ice cubes for?" Alice looked at me with her black eyes, the same kind of orbs on orphans in Keene paintings.

"The cold gets the heart moving. But never mind, we don't need them really, just hand me the salt and the syringe."

With Sam's teaspoon in my hand, I tried to calmly pour a little salt into it. I couldn't really remember exactly how much to use, but there was little time to belabor the question, so I just used an arbitrary amount and put in some tap water, swished it around, and drew this saline solution into the syringe, forgetting about the cotton.

"That works?" Alice demanded.

"That's an antidote?" Tom asked.

"WHAT KIND OF PARTY IS THIS WITH NO BATHROOM FACILITIES!?!" The line was getting riotous.

"SHUT UP AND WAIT!!" Alice screamed at them through the door.

"WAIT?!?! WE'VE BEEN WAITING!!!"

"You're taking too long, Cookie." Tom was wiping the sweat on his forehead with a big beach towel that had a print of a Coca-Cola can on it, with the words "It's The Real Thing."

"He's going to die," Alice was sobbing.

"I told you he's not going to die, Alice!" I said, but I was terrified.

"He'll be brain dead!" Alice screamed and threw herself against the toilet.

"He won't be brain dead either," I said, but I wasn't really sure about that part.

I guess I wasn't too convincing about the brain stuff because Alice started again, "He's going to be a vegetable, no better than a cucumber...he's going to..."

"SHUT UP, ALICE!" I finally screamed, while my hands were shaking trying to find a vein that wasn't too scarred up. I put the syringe's dull point into the only clean vein that I could find, pulled the plunger back, got blood, and then pushed the salt solution into it slowly.

"Is there a possibility he'll be a vegetable?" Tom asked.

"Look, I don't know! But can you imagine Sam a vegetable? Even if he had half a brain he'd be smarter than most of the idiots at this party." This vegetable thing was nagging at all of us.

"WE'RE PISSING IN OUR DRAWERS OUT HERE!" the line screamed.

With my thumb on where his pulse should be, I started getting a little scared about the time it was taking for him to come around. It seemed too long, an eternity. I broke out in beads of sweat. Where was his pulse? He didn't even have a faint one.

"Didn't you know how many bags he did?" Alice turned on Tom. "You could have stopped him!"

BANG, BANG, BANG. The people were pounding on the door. "YOU ASS-HOLES'VE BEEN IN THERE FOR AN HOUR!"

"I didn't know how many he did. How was I supposed to know?" Tom threw the towel on the tiles.

"You jerk! You could have stopped him!" Alice was hysterical.

"How could anybody stop Sam from doing dope?" he screamed.

"At least he was with him, Alice. What if Sam was in here shootin' up all by himself and this happened!" When I said this I felt Sam's pulse returning slightly, then stronger, then some pink came to his face, edging out the blue, and then there was a sudden movement under his eyelids, like his eyeballs were watching some dream go by. In a second his long eyelashes fluttered. He blinked a few times, and opened them.

"Here he comes," I said, relieved. I sunk to the toilet seat because my knees were buckling, they'd no longer hold me. Tom and Alice stopped glaring at each other to look at him.

Sam looked around. His eyes focused and he smiled. He became aware of who was in the room with him.

"Oh, Sam, honey, baby," Alice was kissing him and crying with joy. She was hugging him, leaning way into the cold water so the bustline of her tight satin dress got all wet.

"WOW! That was pretty good stuff! Can we get some more?" Sam asked.

"YOU HAVE TO BE KIDDING!!" Tom wiped the sweat from his face, again with the sleeve of his black sixties silk shirt. He sat down on the floor because his knees had given out too. "You're kidding, right?"

"He's not kidding!" Alice was angry again. "You just O.D.ed, you asshole!"she screamed at Sam.

"You were almost fucking dead, man!" Tom said, laughing nervously.

"I just shot you up with some salt," I said. "Remember it. May come in handy someday."

"How do you feel, Sam, you asshole?" Tom smiled at him. "What an asshole," he said to me happily.

"You had us going there for a while, you jerk," Alice kissed him on his icy lips. "How do you feel?"

"I don't think I'm high anymore, dammit." Sam looked mad. Then he looked down at himself while he sat there in the tub. "Hey! You idiots put me in here with my best sharkskin suit on. You could at least have taken it off me!" He stood up in the tub, dripping and wobbling, "I'm freezing. Could you get me some dry clothes, babe?" he asked Alice.

"Of couse sweetheart," she said and squeezed out the door.

"The two-tone purple one!!" Sam yelled after her.

Somone tried to push in the door when Alice pushed out, but Tom jumped up and stood against it.

"I'M GOING TO PISS RIGHT HERE!" the person said. "I CAN'T HOLD IT ANY LONGER."

"Go ahead!" Sam shouted back to the guy out there, "make yourself at home."

Obviously Sam was not a vegetable. Sam was Sam again, for better or worse. He took off his suit and wrapped himself in the "It's The Real Thing" towel.

Yeah, it sure is, I thought.

Sam's teeth were chattering while he took off the suit and threw it in the corner. He looked kind of pitiful and still wobbly. It seemed like he had shrunk a little. His fingertips were all wrinkled from the water.

"I feel like shit. I'm not even high anymore!" he grumbled.

I left the bathroom. Some people are never happy.

Outside in the living room the party was still jumping. No one had even suspected that the host had practically died a few minutes ago.

In less than five minutes, I saw Sam with a Nebuchadnezzar of champagne,
walking among the dancers, filling people's empty glasses. Someone gave him
another birthday present—the book *Death On the Installment Plan*, by Celine.
Another person handed him a familiar little package, probably more heroin. I
shook my head and fought my way to the kitchen. A filmmaker handed ma a
glass of champagne. I drained it. I remembered that I hated champagne.

"So what have you been doing lately?" this filmmaker asked me.

"Not much," I shrugged, "You know...same old shit...".

A Pathetic Waltz

BY GARY INDIANA

HAD JUST RETURNED FROM COLOMBIA, S.A., WHERE I had been acting in a low budget movie and living in the Hotel Plaza de Bolivar, which is less a hotel than a bordello where cocaine is sold by sordid desk clerks, with the manuscript of my novel, *Burma*, secure in its brown manila folder. I had not written a word of *Burma* in South America, although it had been my intention tow rite a great deal of this book, if not all of it, during the long hiatuses between my acting duties, because I have often acted in films and knew these spells of inactivity would be frequent. The humidity in my room overcame me. I felt confident of finishing *Burma*, for it had started auspiciously, page after page had rolled off my pen, so to speak, with hardly any mental effort, and as it was a book about my own life, my own experience, I thought the detachment and physical distance of South America from the familiar landscape of New York City would enhance my creative efforts. However, the heat and humidity of the Hotel Plaza de Bolivar defeated me. I could not write a word. I lay in bed, under the useless breeze generated by the electric ceiling fan, perspiring, reading again and again the pages that had so easily issued from my earlier flurry of work. With mounting dread I struggled for a phrase, a sentence, a paragraph that could plausibly follow from the point where my novel had broken off, in a summer house in East Hampton. After all, I reasoned, my life continued after that, I'm still alive now, the time that has passed has been rich with incident.

These thoughts gave me confidence. I knew I had done things in life. One experience had followed another, laden with raw material. When I really get to work again on *Burma*, I thought, I'll find that a good deal of germination has taken place. I'm probably still absorbing experiences which I shall be able to use soon. In fact it is probably premature even to contemplate going on, although quite soon I shall go on, continuing from the last paragraph I wrote in East Hampton. And then my own perceptions will surprise me. But not yet.

It had been summer in Colombia, exhaustingly balmy, the damp languourous heat of the day punctured by sudden, torrential rainstorms lasting an hour or so, usually one rainstorm in the morning, another in midafternoon, and a third at the outset of evening. The effect of all these rainstorms, which hardly did anything to abate the deadly heat, was to drench the very air in asphyxiating humidity, so that one felt as if one were breathing water. And when I returned to New York, winter was in full chill. First it was debilitating summer, then demoralizing winter, all within five hours. I boarded the plane in Bogota thinking, at last I can continue with *Burma*, as soon as I'm home in my own flat, among my own belongings, and not in this alien, scorching, sodden environment. When I'm in New York, safely at home, hearing my own language and its inimitable rhythms, words will no lnger fail me. The bracing cold of the New York winter will invigorate my brain.

An exceptionally frigid, wet afternoon greeted me at Kennedy Airport. The Avianca jet landed in a foot of slush, skidding and lurching on the inundated runway. I had been dissuaded from smuggling a small quantity of cocaine by an acquaintance in Cartagena who assured me that everyone entering the United States from Colombia was thoroughly searched by Customs. But the Customs officer waved me through without a glance into my luggage.

In the taxi, I felt the familiar exhilaration of returning to New York, an exhilaration like that of arriving in a completely foreign city, knowing perfectly well that this thrill would soon dissipate, that within a few days my six weeks of tropical escape would become a distant memory. By then, I thought, I'll have resumed *Burma* where I left off, after leaving "Rita"and her summer house four years ago. I had returned to Manhattan then, too, though in summer, not in winter, and without exhilaration, in fact far from any sort of exhilaration. Although in real life I had first gone home for a month, I mean to my family's home in New Hampshire, and then back to Manhattan, I had decided in *Burma* to leave out this depressing episode, as one is entitled in fiction, for the sake of artistry, to change certain elements and leave out certain episodes which do nothing to further one's general design. And the month I had spent in real life, at home wtih my aging parents, between leaving Rita and resuming my existence in Manhattan, had no place at all in the general design of *Burma*, far from it. A description of this period, in my view, would simply have depressed and alienated anyone, including myself. No, best to edit this family visit right out of *Burma*, ploughing ahead with the central story.

I arrived at my apartment house, grateful for the small weight of my bags. For once I had not overpacked or acquired heavy books during the journey. In Colombia I had purchased nothing, and the only additions to the luggage I'd left New York with were four large conch shells and a lump of brain coral that I pulled from the surf in the Rosario Islands. And despite these supplementary baggage items, various parts of my wardrobe had been left behind, with the film's wardrobe mistress, in the event that it became necessary to re-shoot scenes and hence to return to Cartagena. This clothing had weighed roughly the same as the shells in my luggage, and so I returned carrying virtually the same amount that I'd left with.

Within a few hours, the customary hopelessness of my apartment had succeeded, as it always did, in ruining the optimistic mood of the flight and the taxi ride. There has never been adequate storage space in this narrow flat, nor have I ever been able to control the insane proliferation of papers, books, magazines, clothing, shoes, furniture and broken machines such as tape recorders and radios, the sheer accumulation of detritus in this flat has always defeated me and ruined any bright mood I might bring in from outside. Not that the flat itself is particularly gloomy. On the contrary, others have long envied the ample sunlight this apartment enjoys, if that is the word, and the disarray which has always caused me disorientation and actual grief has never bothered other people, who quite often claim, when I apologize for it, to live in a disorder so far exceeding my own disorder that mine seems to them the spirit of tidiness, a claim that has always sounded to me like a brazen lie. But it is true, of course, that the disorder of others often appears orderly to oneself. One cannot necessarily imagine a better order for other people's belongings, since they are usually of little interest or importance to oneself. It seems to me, though, that my own disorder, which is far from intentional, demonstrates the impossibilty of maintaining any state of order whatsoever in a city where disorder is the norm, where one is never left alone for a single minute, and where importunity reigns supreme. For ten years, since moving here from a different city, I have been continually inconvenienced and importuned by other people, not the people with whom I choose to spend time, but others, other people whom I hardly know and have no connection with, people who want things and who view others as implements, tools, and opportunities. One cannot help being shocked, as a resident of such a city, by the flagrant usury, if that is the word, employed by persons who know what they want and are willing to use anyone and everyone in order to advance their venal, obnoxious designs. A person living in such a place may easily find himself the object of grotesque attentions from people who want things, without soliciting such attentions in any fashion whatever. For even a few days to pass without the intrusion of phone calls and letters from the craven individuals who infest this city is to know inner peace of an unprecedented kind. But I have never known such peace, since moving here, except during the three or four days after my return from a journey, when people believe I am still away. After three or four days the word gets around, and the circus of importunity resumes with renewed malignancy. People who have never understood the writer's intrinsic and irrefutable need for solitude and peace, who have never understood and will never understand such a need, constantly attack the writer's precious solitude with every sort of cunning.

After returning from Colombia, I did, in fact, experience several days of uninterrupted calm. But the dispiriting mess of my cramped flat paralyzed me. My desk, which has never really been neat, was strewn with bills, letters, pencils, stamps, note pads, matchbooks, the chamber of a lock I had replaced some months earlier, loose pages of a journal I was unable to keep longer than a week, paperback books, and all the other distracting objects that reduce the mind's ability to concentrate. This mess was destroying me, destroying my mind and destroying *Burma*, despite the otherwise ideal conditions that prevailed in the immediate wake of my return.

For several days the deliquescence of the apartment impeded my progress. Why had I never taken energetic steps against the inevitable decay and clutter, the dense piling-up of increasingly impersonal effects, in all the many years I had lived in this far from ideal, but somehow inevitable residence? I had taken some steps, but not enough. Whatever measures I took were neutralized and overtaken by the action of time. The building was falling apart, year by year. The wooden floors were decayed. The brick walls leak plaster dust over every surface. Everything crumbles. It's impossible to move anywhere, since even a smaller place would now be twice as expensive. Whenever I returned from a journey I found myself freshly disturbed to consider that I might have to live in such a crumbling, narrow, inconvenient flat for the rest of my life, or at least for as long as I lived in Manhattan. Which is, as far as I'm concerned, the same thing as being sentenced to life imprisonment. Why should a human being inhabit the same apartment for twenty, thirty, forty years? What influence does such a term of imprisonment exert on the human brain, what crushing limitations are imposed by such a term of imprisonment?

This line of thought led me nowhere. Recalling my sanguine mood upon checking out of the Hotel Plaza de Bolivar, I resolved on putting things in order. Once things were in order, thse black thoughts could find no fertile ground. After some hours my desk, except for the typewriter and a stack of typing paper, was bare and polished. I turned on the radio, tuning it to a classical music station, arranged my cigarettes and matches near the typewriter, sat down, rolled a blank sheet into the typewriter, lighted a cigarette, and stared. I had been so long away from *Burma* that a glow of anticipation actually made my skin tingle.

Burma broke off as the narrator prepared to enter East Hampton. Four years earlier I, too, had left East Hampton, under similar but not identical circumstances. Though drawn from my own life, *Burma* was not entirely my own story, its narrator's obsessions were not my obsessions. I had invented the book-within-the-book, the never-quite-remembered story, and my plan, as far as I could recall, had been to connect the climax of the book with the climax of the book-within-the-book, in the process sorting through the confused intervening years. Since the period of the book I had contributed a number of essays to a number of publications. I had established myself, to some extent, as a writer, I no longer lived entirely like a marginal person. Yet, on the other hand, I had not achieved anything resembling independence, my inner life continued fluctuating between hope and negation, so to speak. *Burma* was addressed to a "You" that I had once been desperately infatuated with and now felt nothing but indifference toward, for reasons that are too tangled and ultimately too tiresome to enumerate. Therefore the problem I now faced, the *Burma* problem, consisted in recapturing defunct feelings, recapturing and then transposing them to an imaginary object. This "You" of *Burma*, the addressee, so to speak, had been present to my writing mind no later than two months earlier, and yet, and yet, "You" seemed now, as I looked over the manuscript, less than entirely present, and not simply less than entirely present but an almost grotesquely inappropriate, hypothesized reader of *Burma*. But to expunge this "You" clearly meant to destroy the very form of *Burma*, "You" couldn't just be done away with so easily. *I will simply pretend that You is someone else,* I decided, turning up the manuscript's last page and scrutinizing its last words, *enjoyed a state of truce.*

I decided to fix a pot of coffee, for sustained alertness during the creative act. The kitchen yielded an almost empty bag of Bustelo coffee, a saucepan, filter papers; I boiled water, then poured it over the mingy tablespoon of Bustelo. A trickle of brackish water dribbled into the glass pot. This won't do, I realized: what I need to get going is a full, robust, nerve-shattering pot of coffee, rather than this tepid stream of nauseating liquid, which resembles the *tinto* sold in medicine cups in the streets of Cartagena.

Though I had enjoyed that mild beverage in Cartagena, I had no wish to enjoy it here. I dressed in several layers of warm clothing, and went out, braving the arc tic cold. The day, however, was bright. People of all sorts trampled through the streets, in heavy boots, stamping through puddles of grimy slush. Snow melted ubiquitously. I had dressed for bitter weather. But the sun shone, the air was warm. I walked several blocks, down Second Avenue, my spirits lifting. I drank in the mixture of old and new sights. For years now, the slum neighborhood I inhabit has been changing into a fashionable district, the result of a supposed artistic renaissance in the area, and of all the corruption and hypocrisy this implies, the professional classes, ever intent on living amid novelty, have bought all the property in this so-called bohemian sector, driving out the city's poorest inhabitants. Everything shining and new in this neighborhood reminds me that soon it will be impossible for anyone except the rich to live here. In spite of this repulsive process, which nothing can stop or even slightly delay, my depression evaporated at the sight of so much vile, meaningless activity, and the transformations effected during my sojourn in South America. It is curious, but one can, if necessary, find solace in repulsive things. And this is especially true in this neighborhood, for some reason.

These streets with their low buildings, tenements and storefronts had once contained the mystery of *Burma*: I lived in them, but thought of someone on another continent who wandered rootless through the world, sometimes intercepting me in my travels. I met him not long after leaving East Hampton, he became my emotional history for three years, notwithstanding my attempts to break free or to interest myself in other people who were more accessible; I did, in fact, make a fool of myself with a number of other foolish people, but it all came out to nothing. And now it was all long over with and I was, in a manner of speaking, free. The clean slate of the day with its gouged and scarred pentimento of other days, nights, weeks, decades was my clean slate,and the air was blue, clear, only slightly cool, almost a spring air, as if washed by the newly fallen, rapidly melting snow. There are no seasons any more *per se*. It only remained for the evenings to grow morbid near Christmas Eve, melancholy around New Year's, symbolically bright at Eastertime.

In a Korean vegetable market near 5th Street, I buy a fresh bag of coffee and cream, noticing that my funds are dissolving as rapidly and unconsciously as ever. And there I see Victor, rooting around amid the anise root and cabbages, holding a green plastic shopping basket stuffed with produce and dairy products. I call to him. He turns, surprised to see me, dropping a large turnip into a watery basin of tofu patties. We embrace awkwardly. He retrieves his turnip. Victor's wearing a light denim jacket with fleecy white lining, his curly brown hair is clipped short, his glasses make his smooth face look square. I think I've known Victor as long as I've lived in New York. Ordinarily, I see Victor every few days, or speak to Victor on the telephone, I suppose in the last years nothing much has ever happened to me without Victor knowing about it, though Victor is less forthcoming about what happens to him. Perhaps I am less curious about Victor's experiences than Victor is about mine, I ask Victor less often than he asks me: What's going on with you, how are you feeling, what's bothering you, are you all right, have you been feeling better. So I have kept Victor aware of my vicissitudes as if he absolutely needed to know every trivial thing that happened to me, and of course now that I think of it this must have required considerable forbearance on Victor's part over the years. After all the myriad trips—not myriad really, but many—trips I have taken, I contacted Victor. I used to talk about my journeys, but no more. And after returning from South America I refrained from contacting Victor or anyone else, with the exception of my mother, who lives in a small town and has done so all her life, and hence frets and worries over my travels in what she calls the big wide world, though of course there is nothing to worry about. We shall all be dead soon enough, one way or another. From my mother there is little danger of disruption in my routine. For twenty years I have phoned my mother every Sunday. For twenty years, my mother has only phoned me when a death occurs in our family, or when I have failed to call for several weeks. No one in my family expects the slightest thing from anyone else in my family, since the family dreams of my mother and father were shattered long ago. Not all at once, but in increments. First my father went deaf, then alcoholic. Next, my mother's favorite brother died from cancer of the throat, a death that dragged on and on for years and years, causing this once handsome, alert man to become a drunkard and a walking cadaver, his appearance mutilated by repeated surgery. Later my brother married a woman whose hostility toward my family cast a pall over my brother's visits, which became less and less frequent as time passed. And I myself, after leaving home for college in a large city, went completely mad, being unable to cope with the discovery that nothing in my background had prepared me for real life, and that I was doomed like everyone else. For two years, I had a series of breakdowns, and was carted in and out of the nearest mental hospital like a piece of furniture. When that period finished, I wasted ten years in a trance of incessant motion and meaningless employment, in ever more remote cities, thus destroying whatever hopes my parents had entertained for me. As soon as my situation stabilized, a tumor was found in my father's intestines, requiring extensive surgery, then chemotherapy. My father's cancer treatment forced him to stop drinking, which he had done excessively since going deaf. When he stopped drinking his hearing returned, as it might have done thirty-five years earlier, had he stopped drinking then. My father's despair, which had formed so much of the atmosphere of my childhood and my brother's childhood, left him suddenly at the age of sixty. Then, quite predictably, my mother became alcoholic as my father's health and disposition improved. As my father's despair lessened, my mother's despair grew. Throughout my childhood, my father lived in a world of silence and despair, totally dependent upon my mother. Now my mother became dependent on alcohol, no longer needing to maintain her strength. She became weak as he became strong. These are by no means the only miseries which ruined the hopes and dreams of my family, only a few, typical miseries such as beset and ruin every family. I don't know why I mention them, really.

A person never frees himself entirely from the sad history of such miseries, naturally. A person can only hope to confine his reflections or wallowings to some formally regulated routine, and my weekly phone call, assuaging my mother's anxiety over my supposedly dangerous travels, served this purpose. Since I had not called my mother from South America, I called her and talked for an unusually long time when I returned. But I didn't let anyone else know I was again in my apartment. My ambition to complete, or at least resume *Burma* demanded the silence of a few days, but of course one cannot leave one's apartment in such circumstances, since doing so risks the chance encounter. But I left anyway, walking directly into an encounter with Victor. I now wonder how many works of literary creation have failed to materialize, thanks to the kind of unforeseen distraction I let myself in for that day, over a year ago, by leaving my apartment.

But what does it matter now? I had only to tell Victor that I was working assiduously, against tremendous odds. Instead, if memory serves, we drank coffee in a Mexican restaurant. I related my South American adventures. Victor described his recent efforts at painting (he had given this up for several years). The sunlight glared and shimmered on the waxy red tablecloth. When I closed my eyes I imagined myself on the dining room terrace of the Hotel Plaza de Bolivar, staring into a glass of the wretched local wine and thinking about *Burma* and the sequence of real-life events that followed from the final paragraph to the seedy hotel terrace in that crumbling Caribbean port. From the terrace one could see the huge carved doors of the Palace of the Inquisition. I looked into Victor's eyes, brown and watery behind the thick lenses of his horn-rimmed glasses. The terrace faded into the frost-smeared plate glass facing Second Avenue.

I was not in South America anymore. *This wretched town*—Victor said, reminding me of all the miseries living here had piled on over time. I could remember a time, not long before this, when everything had seemed possible, and wondered how it had come about that within a short time everything became impossible and out of the question. A person is young, he thinks anything can happen, and everything does happen, and even after making every conceivable mistake, things still appear laden with possibility. A few years go by, and everything is a mistake, everything becomes impossible, any step turns out to be a mistake, any action causes despair and horror. Victor, for example, had come to New York in his youth, to become an artist, and instead fell into furniture design, to support himself. And soon every type of person wanted Victor's furniture, to sit on Victor's chairs and recline on Victor's sofas, in their so-called gracious homes. Victor hates making furniture, yet this is precisely what he is valued for, making things he despises and cannot stop making. A person is young, he thinks he'd rather starve than do things he hates, to keep alive, to keep alive. And naturally by keeping alive this way, he isn't alive, he is living but he isn't alive. He is only keeping alive his albuminous substance, dragging it from one impossible situation to the next like a sack weighted down with iron filings.

On this rare day in December, with a clear head, I understood all this, without forming any conclusion. I could not have endured another day of solitude, *Burma* notwithstanding, and despite every resolve to become methodical, disciplined, and single-minded about my own concerns. In the vast stream of time, my own concerns were doomed to vanish without a trace like everyone else's. Victor's problems would also be flushed down the toilet of passing time. *This is a banner year*, I said, and Victor surprised me by agreeing without asking what I meant. We drank more coffee. The sun had started fading. I felt my will dissolve. Any day now, I thought, I shall have to look for money, and I've exhausted every source. I said it aloud. Victor said, You'll have to write something, then. If I write something, I said, for a magazine, for instance, I won't be paid for months and months, and you can never make enough to live, writing, and besides, I said, I've nothing whatsoever to say, I've hardly said anything but at the same time I've said more than enough, as far as I'm concerned. Everything I want to do is much too complicated for my brain.

You'll see, Victor said. Things are going to change now, very quickly. I'm fed up with everything, personally. When people are fed up, things change.

Not necessarily, I said. I remember exactly one year ago, we were sitting in a place like this, not drinking coffee but beer. I had just published a quite long essay on the philosopher Wittgenstein, and I recall being thoroughly fed up with everything, and if memory serves, you were fed up with everything as well. Your life, your work, your relationship with Richard which even then you characterized as unrewarding and masochistic, and look here, I went on, nothing whatsoever has really happened. I went to Europe four times on other people's money, and now I've gone to South America. But I've accomplished nothing in all this. You, meanwhile, continue to make furniture, see the same friends, and still go out with Richard, which is anyway something. I carried the torch for three years for Alexis, and probably spent a total of ten evenings in bed with Alexis, most of them in different countries and spaced out over months, now I'm almost thirty-five and I've wasted the last part of my youth on someone who didn't love me, and what's even worse, in my estimation, is that nothing has changed since this time last year. Except that we've both gotten older and possibly even more deluded than we were at this time a year ago.

What do you mean deluded? I'm disgusted, not deluded. If I were deluded I'd still be happy, Victor declared.

When were you ever happy, I challenged. Victor, I've known you for years, you have always been unnaturally agreeable but I'm quite certain you have never been happy for a single moment.

I've had moments of unhappiness, Victor said, but that isn't what I meant. I was less unhappy when I wasn't aware of how things sit. As you get older you see how things go, how things work, and what makes the world go around. And then you're really in for it.

Someday we'll both think we were happy right now, I said, I'm sure of it.

And I was, absolutely sure. You go along dissatisfied at all times with everything, becoming bored and exhausted even with the few things you could once tolerate, and naturally look back believing you were happier once upon a time, though this question of happy or not happy is quite ridiculous. If I think about then, that day, wasting time with Victor, I see *Burma* breaking away from my mind as a large chunk of a glacier might break away from the entire mass and float away irretrievably. Was it then, that day, when I realized an *inner blankness* had truly replaced the gnarled, impossible feelings that had dominated me for three years, that I had at last achieved a state of suspension, a condition of feeling nothing or almost nothing, in which the past of *Burma*, the *Burma* past, was insubstantial, invalid, a history of youthful detours and sidetracks? If not that precise afternoon, then at roughly that period, the pre-Christmas period, the feeling of persisting in the face of error began to melt away. I began to see clearly the warped patterns that had influenced my comings and goings in the world, the egregious and increasingly extravagant methods of escape I had employed to avoid facing things. I had, for example, agreed to the South American trip in order to avoid *Burma*, convincing myself that travel would enrich my consciousness, when in fact it had done nothing of the sort, it had simply distracted me from my own self-set goals, my own aspirations. It had also put my mind off my three-year mania for Alexis and enabled me—this was the positive side, really—to conclude this unfavorable, punishing, three-year long relationship in my own mind. When I returned from South America, Alexis no longer existed for me. Or rather, he existed, but nothing more than that. No longer would I pine away and suffer because of him, far from it. I had never occupied that much of his attention, whereas he had occupied nearly all of my attention, had in fact permeated my every waking and unconscious thought, I had been hopelessly and absurdly in love with Alexis whereas, for Alexis, I hardly existed at all. And now he hardly existed at all for me. Alexis was out of my system, just as I had always been more or less out of his system. Even if I hadn't made the slightest progress on *Burma*, my trip had achieved the important purpose of putting Alexis out of my mind. However, Alexis had inspired *Burma* and now I could not go on with *Burma* as I had intended, everything would have to change.

Therefore part of the problem, as I then thought, was, *Burma* minus Alexis. And what about me minus Alexis, would that be genuinely liberating, or another trap? You go on and on in all futility with someone, utterly dissatisfied, thinking to save yourself by getting rid of him, then you get rid of him and find you have nothing left. You have no one to think about, no focus for your cogitations. And therefore the whole meaning of your life disappears, despair sets in, sometimes followed by suicide.

These speculations flashed through my thoughts in less than a moment. I dismissed them as jejune. Alexis had been as much of a mental construction as *Burma*, an obsession no one else could possibly experience, least of all Alexis. In some senses it was absolutely worthless because it was, had been, impalpable and baseless. The proof being that I no longer felt anything about it, and nothing in the world could possibly make it exist again, least of all Alexis, about whom I now felt nothing whatsoever. He existed as before, but I felt nothing about him. Strange. He existed no more and no less than he had when his existence meant everything to me.

Some weeks later, Victor said, *You know something, you haven't mentioned Alexis in quite a long time.* But by then something else had started happening, if anything more consuming and ridiculous than what had gone before.

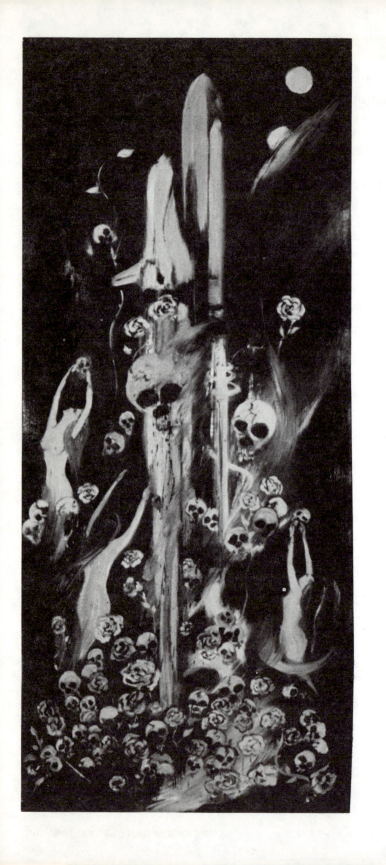

St. Marks' Horror

BY DAVID POLONOFF

ON JANUARY 2, 1986, DONALD BRADSTREET, attorney with the firm of Cardigan & Crumwell, his wife Tricia, account executive for Chaste Manhattan Securities, their two children and Akita moved into a renovated duplex at 666 St. Marks Place. Two months later they fled in terror. This is their story.

December 1985—Donald spotted the ad in the *Journal* and contacted the agent. Tricia said it was a 'hot property.' The agent informed them of the building's history. Originally a tenement inhabited largely by Hispanic families, it had been torched by the super's pyromaniac son and fallen into the hands of neighborhood drug addicts. In recent years it had been partially restored by a group of performance artists. The Bradstreets were unconcerned. The renovators had done their job well. The huge plate glass windows and high-gloss floors offered a protective shield against an unsavory past...

January 2, 1986—Donald settled with the movers. As he put away his American Express card, he noticed a sweet, pungent odor. He switched on the ultrasonic humidifier. The smell grew stronger. He remembered his pre-law days at the dorm. Cannabis! In his co-op! Trish and Don ran from room to room searching for its source. They never found it. For the next two months that stench would be their constant companion.

Jan. 4—Don couldn't sleep. He heard something that sounded like music. The same three chords, incessantly repeating. He tiptoed to the living room. The CD player was off. It grew still. Trish awoke as Don was throwing his Burberry over his pajamas. He gave her a trancelike stare. "This place is dead. I'm going to the Wah Wah."

Jan. 5—Tricia dreamed that the bathtub was in the kitchen.

Jan. 7—Five-year-old Jennifer removed the Akita's collar and put it on.

Jan. 8—Trish was in the basement doing laundry when she discovered a hidden room. She called Don. It was a dank, chill place and reeked of domestic beer. Its walls were swathed with lurid day-glo images. "This must have been their performance space," said Don in hushed tones. Trish had a vision of ghoulishly made-up figures performing weird acts of self-mutilation and destruction, shrieking, writhing, chanting, while a black-clad audience stood by impassively, watching . . . from that day on they sent their laundry to a service.

Jan. 10—Marshall, the Bradstreet's three-year-old, refused to eat his pasta. "If you don't finish your dinner, you won't get Tofutti," Trish reprimanded. Marshall began to vomit a heavy green fluid. Yet the pasta had not been pesto.

Jan. 12—The Bradstreets awoke to find the walls of their co-op covered with graffiti. Tricia started yelling at the kids. "But Mommy," protested Marshall, "that's not my tag!"

That evening a heavily accented man in Armani clothes appeared on the front door TV monitor. He said he was a European collector and left his card. The Bradstreets never saw him again.

Jan. 15—Donald dreamed he had passed up an investment opportunity and woke up screaming. Trembling, he described the nightmare to Trish. From somewhere deep in her throat came a voice he had never heard before: "It's only money, dear."

Jan. 16—Trish asked Don to tie her to the futon frame.

Jan. 18—The Bradstreets ordered Chinese takeout. Opening the boxes, they gasped in mute horror. The rice was yellow and smothered with black beans. The mixed vegetables consisted of mashed potatoes with mushroom gravy and canned peas and carrots. There was no broccoli!

Jan. 21—Jennifer was drawing pictures on the Macintosh. Marshall was babbling contentedly. Suddenly, he started screaming out in some incomprehensible tongue. Don and Trish rushed to his room. "Yo!" said the toddler, "loose joints."

Jan. 24—Tricia reached for a spoon to toss the tortellini salad. Ouch! It was red hot. A whitish liquid bubbled on its surface. She pulled another spoon from the drawer. A soggy piece of cotton clung to it! She dumped out the drawer. All her Dansk silver was bent and charred, and blackened as if singed from an invisible match.

Jan. 25—Marshall: Sense! Crack! Dimes!

Don: Where did you learn those words?

Marsh: José taught me.

Don: Who's José?

Marsh: My main man.

Don: And just what does José do?

Marsh (pointing to corner): Why don't you ask him, daddy?

Don turned to where his son had pointed. He thought he saw a figure disappearing in the shadows.

Jan. 28—Tricia had just called Dial-a-car. As she went to get her attaché case, she had the sensation of levitating. Looking down she was horrified to find six-inch stiletto heels where her Reeboks had been. She wobbled over to the mirror—her mouth was smeared with purple lipstick.

Feb. 1—Trish put *Jane Fonda's Workout* on the VCR. The tape seemed to take possession of her body. Suddenly a rasping voice ordered her to turn her head in a 360-degree circle. Don stopped her just in time.

Feb. 4—Don went to the kitchen for a midnight snack. A gooey yellow substance covered the Italian tile floor. Brie! He struggled over to the counter. It was still running!

Feb. 5—Don said work was boring.

Feb. 7—Trish was absorbed in her Sony Walkman when a terrible din invaded her private space. Barging into her son's room, she found him dressed in sunglasses and a black turtleneck, banging on bongos. She barely recognized Jennifer through the hair extensions. Horror clutched at her throat: the Akita's fur was crimson and shaved in a full-body mohawk!

"José said we needed a look," said Marshall.

Feb. 9—Don didn't shower after running. He spent the day in his sweats, playing CD disks and watching the soaps.

Feb. 12—Trish and Don sat in front of the Toshiba watching *St. Elsewhere.* Jennifer scurried about the living room picking things up. A few minutes later they saw her heading for the door with a bulging Charivari bag. Don looked inside. It was filled with clothes, records and houseware. "Why are you taking our possessions out to the street?' he asked, aghast.

"José told me to sell them."

Feb. 13—Don was still wearing his sweats.

Feb. 14—Valentine's Day! In the past it would have meant Krön for Trish and KL Homme for Don. But the heart of darkness had descended on the Bradstreet home.

Trish wondered if they should seek counseling.

Feb. 15—Don played Lotto with money from profit-sharing.

Feb. 16—Trish found *In Search of Excellence* in the trash compactor.

Feb. 19—Don finally took off his sweat suit. When Trish came home, he was standing in front of the mirror in her best Laura Ashley.

Feb. 21—Jennifer found cockroaches in her croissant.

Feb. 22—The Akita contracted a sexually transmitted disease.

Feb. 23—Trish woke up too late for brunch.

Feb. 24—Don looked for gossip columns in the Sunday *Times*.

Feb. 25—Trish found syringes and cold pizza in the Ficus planter.

Feb. 26—A shadow man appeared on the wall.

Feb. 27—Marshall traded his Gobots for a ghetto blaster.

Feb. 28—Don said the sushi was overcooked.

March 1—The horror! The horror!

March 2—The Cremina-Olympia espresso machine hissed malevolently. Gelato oozed from the Simac, forming a pulsating blob which advanced upon the Bradstreets. Terror-stricken, they fled into the bedroom, slamming the French doors just in time to avoid the razor-sharp linguini which La Machine spit forth at them.

Fissures snaked across the floor-to-ceiling windows. The IBM PC slamdanced with the exposed brick walls. Huge shards of polyurethane ripped themselves free of the floor. Glassine bags and drink tickets fell from the ceiling.

"This co-op is possessed!" wailed Trish. "Let's cut our losses!"

They grabbed the kids and headed downstairs.

A man blocked the front stoop with a velvet rope.

"You're not on the guest list," he said.

The Bradstreets retreated upstairs. Don pushed open the living room door. A crowd of zombies jammed every available space, sipping white wine. It was an opening, Don's opening! His fifteen minutes were up. They threw their cheese and crackers on the floor and huddled in the corner, whispering, screeching, gnawing, creeping on rodent feet back to nibble on the cheese. They were a giant rat which stared Don in the face and said, "Scram!"

"Take your damned building, tax-deductible maintenance and all!" howled Don.

He felt purged. Everything grew calm.

Epilogue: Parapsychologists agree that human beings use only a fraction of their mental powers. In the East Village this is especially true. Its many generations of bohemians, misfits, and immigrants have left their psychic imprint on their surroundings. Renovation has done much to exorcise this unholy presence, but some condos may never be fit for civilized habitation. The Bradstreets are now living incognito somewhere in the Trump Tower. They warn prospective co-opers that Loisaida holds secrets which the upwardly mobile were not meant to know.

List of Illustrations

front
cover   Martin Wong, *La Viera de Nuyorico*. Oil on canvas, collection Joel Cooper.
page vi   Anton Van Dalen, 1983. Photocopy, collection artist.
pagex   Seth Tobacman. Crayon and collage on paper, collection artist.
page 2   Keiko Bonk, *Blind Love*. Oil on canvas, collection artist.
page 10   Keiko Bonk, *Little Wing*, 1986. Acrylic on paper.
page 14   Anton Van Dalen, stencils, 1981. Photocopy, collection artist.
page 16   Martin Wong, *Upstate Annunciation (Cupcake & Paco)*. Oil on canvas, collection Syracuse University (gift of Christopher Dark).
page 20   Anton Van Dalen, *Los Amigos*, 1977. Pencil on paper, collection artist.
page 22   Keiko Bonk, *Study for Mom*. Oil on canvas, collection artist.
page 34   Martin Wong, *Everlast*, 1988. Oil on canvas, collection of Patrick Bannon, New York.
page 46   Martin Wong, *Orion*, 1984. Collection Ace Baumgold.
page 60   Bobby G (Robert Goldman), *Choppers Over the Projects*, 1981. Acrylic on paper, collection Kiki Smith.
page 64   Anton Van Dalen, stencil, 1981. Photocopy, collection artist.
page 68   Keiko Bonk, *Love Club* 1986. Ink on paper.
page 72   Keiko Bonk, *Love the One You're With*, 1985. Oil on canvas.
page 76   Anton Van Dalen, *Falling House*, 1976. Pencil on paper.
page 105   Martin Wong, *Elena's Storefront*, 1986. Oil on canvas
page 106   Anton Van Dalen, *Abandoned Car with TV and Dog*, 1977. Pencil on paper.
page 116   Martin Wong, after Jorge Brandon's (aka. El Coco Que Habla) painted doorway.
page 128   Martin Wong, *Big Heat (Hypnos & Thanotos)*. Oil on canvas.
page 136   Keiko Bonk.
page 146   Robert Hawkins, *Green Mamba with Candle*. Oil on canvas, collection artist.
page 164   Keiko Bonk, *Toys*, 1985. Oil on canvas.

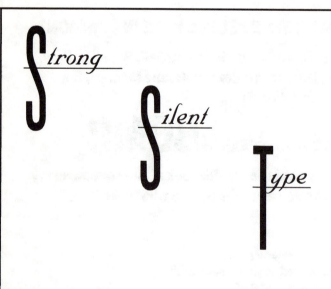

Additional Semiotext(e) / Autonomedia Titles

COLUMBUS & OTHER CANNIBALS
THE WÉTIKO DISEASE & THE WHITE MAN
JACK D. FORBES

A noted American Indian scholar and activist
examines the heritage of indigenous American
cultures since the coming of Europeans in the
15th century, with a particular focus on the
"wétiko disease," the White Man's fascination
with the exploitation and control of nature
and his fellow man.
Spring, 1991 — $12 postpaid

"GONE TO CROATAN"
ORIGINS OF AMERICAN DROPOUT CULTURE
JAMES KOEHNLINE & PETER LAMBORN WILSON, EDITORS

Studies of lost American history and the cultures
of disappearance, including "tri-racial isolate"
communities, the bucaneers, "white Indians,"
black Islamic movements, the Maroons of the
Great Dismal Swamp, scandalous eugenics
theories, rural "hippie" communes, and many other
aspects of American autonomous cultures.
A *festschrift* in honor of historian Hugo Leaming
Bey of the Moorish Science Temple.
Spring, 1991 — $12 postpaid

TROTSKYISM AND MAOISM
THEORY AND PRACTICE IN FRANCE & THE U.S.A.
A. BELDEN FIELDS

An important examination of the critical heritage
of Trotsky and Mao in two Western national
contexts, focusing on the multitudinous parties
and sects and their positions on national and
international issues, racism, sexism, party / worker
positions, gay rights, and students movements.
Charts of organizational histories.
Now Available — $12 postpaid

MODEL CHILDREN
MY SOVIET SUMMERS AT ARTEK
PAUL THOREZ

The son of long-time French Communist Party
chief Maurice Thorez recounts his post-war
childhood experiences at Artek, the prestigious
Crimean summer camp for children of the Soviet
elite, where he saw aspects of Russian political
culture rarely revealed to the West.
Photos and Maps.
Now Available — $12 postpaid

Additional Semiotext(e) / Autonomedia Titles

XEROX PIRATES
"HIGH" TECH & THE NEW COLLAGE UNDERGROUND
AUTONOMEDIA COLLECTIVE, EDITORS

Art and politics meet in heady ways in this amazing and incendiary collection of work in the "high" tech medium of photocopy collage. Post-surrealist traditions of oneiric reverie meet the radical hard-edge of "détourned" advertisements and other recuperations of the mass-mediated image. Works by many well-known marginal artists like Winston Smith, James Koehnline, Dadata, Freddie Baer, Anti-Authoritarians Anonymnous, Sue Ann Harkey.
Spring, 1991 — $14 postpaid

FILM & POLITICS IN THE THIRD WORLD
JOHN DOWNING, EDITOR

The only anthology of its kind in English, with critical articles — most of them written by Third World writers — on leading figures and national cinemas, including analyses of important single films, political/aesthetic manifestoes, and interviews with directors from Africa, China, India, Turkey, Iran, the Arab World, the Philippines, Cuba, Latin America, and more.
Now Available — $12 postpaid

AESTHETICS OF DISAPPEARANCE
PAUL VIRILIO

From infantile narcolepsy to the illusion of
movement in speed, the author of *Pure War*
and *Speed and Politics* and other works examines
the "aesthetic" of disappearance: in film,
in politics, in war, in the philosophy of
subjectivity, and elsewhere.
Now Available — $12 postpaid

CLIPPED COINS, ABUSED WORDS, AND CIVIL GOVERNMENT
JOHN LOCKE'S PHILOSOPHY OF MONEY
CONSTANTINE GEORGE CAFFENTZIS

Starting from the political crisis arising from the
"clipping" of silver currency by monetary pirates
in 17th-century England, Caffentzis opens out
into an original and very provocative critique
of John Locke's economic beliefs, his theories
of language, and his philosophy of history
and the state. Virtually all of the standard critical
work on Locke is "undone" through Caffentzis'
ampliative treatment—which also extends to
intervene in the leading debates in the
monetary theories of the present day.
Now Available — $12 postpaid